5.95

ox/oa Aug 29/95

D0687866

The Sporting News

SELECTS

STOCK CAR RACING'S 50 GREATEST DRIVERS

A Celebration of the All-Time Best

Published by The Sporting News, 10176 Corporate Square Drive, Suite 200, St. Louis, MO 63132.

The Sporting News is a federally regisistered trademark of Vulcan Sports Media, Inc. Visit our website at www.sportingnews.com.

ISBN: 0-89204-664-3

The SportingNews

SELECTS

STOCK CAR RACING'S 50 GREATEST DRIVERS

CONTENTS

When a race finally gets going, maneuvering into and out of the pit area is a key to a driver's mastery of the track.

inevitable setbacks that will occur along the way. Spinouts, damaged cars, bad pit stops, or a bad set of tires will test a driver's mental toughness, and the ability to bounce back and to realistically readjust expectations is an essential skill.

The final element of race strategy is the aggression factor. Good drivers know how to make it clear that they have a superior car, and they know when to demonstrate that superiority to key opponents. The ultimate goal is to get in position to win, which can involve anything from leading as many laps as possible with a great car to being able to milk a late caution flag to pull off an unexpected win or a solid finish.

5. Track Mastery

Being a good driver means knowing how to run well on as many different kinds of tracks as possible. It means knowing how to read the air in the draft, how to avoid getting shuffled back in the pack and how to pick draft partners. It means knowing how to save brakes, use sheet metal and the chrome horn on a short track and being able to get around a tricky groove on a flat track. It means knowing how to pick the right line on a speedway, and which techniques to use to get through corners on a road course, which are very different from the tactics used on any other kind of track.

Knowing the track also involves being able to use the weather conditions to get the most out of the car, and to use the weather as an advantage when conditions begin to deteriorate. The final element of track mastery is getting onto and out of pit road—knowing the pitfalls at each track and the kinds of adjustments that are often required can help a crew chief and pit crew save valuable time, and it makes it easier for them to adjust the car effectively as well.

information, they can translate it effectively to the crew chief, a communication process that facilitates the best possible calls and adjustments during the race.

The variable that can throw a monkey wrench into even the best race strategy is the

6. Knowing and Saving the Equipment

In the early days of NASCAR, virtually every driver was an owner/operator. Drivers were as familiar with the guts of the car as the chief mechanics who doubled as crew chiefs, and they had a far greater knowledge of what had to be done to take care of the equipment (which was far more volatile and fragile than it is today).

As the cars have become more technically sophisticated and split-second precision on pit stops has gotten more essential to winning races, the driver's level of knowledge of the car has changed dramatically. Today's drivers probably know far less about the technical side of the car, but the good ones still know the parameters of the tire and how to save brakes and tires at tracks where that issue is relevant, and they know how far they can push the motor at different points in the race. In general, most good drivers approach the issue of car knowledge by looking for a balance between having the right amount of technical knowledge and having a feel for the car, combining those factors into their race strategy to get into position to win.

7. Building a Team

While the owner/operator has become a bit of a dinosaur on the NASCAR racing landscape, there have been a few drivers whose achievements in this area have been noteworthy, and in some cases monumental. The most significant, of course, are Richard Petty, who founded a racing dynasty as a driver, and Dale Earnhardt, who was able to spin off his highly successful racing company, DEI, after learning the ropes from Richard Childress, who was himself a former driver.

The skill set necessary to be a successful owner/operator is very far from the talent required to be a good driver, and there's also a significant difference in skills in being a successful

Dale Earnhardt, taking a stroll with Jeff Gordon, knew what it took to build a racing team and develop chemistry.

owner/operator at different levels. Some of NASCAR's best racing has been provided by smaller owner/operators with the financial acumen, equipment knowledge and ability to judge racing talent, both in terms of the driver and team members. Prime recent examples include Ricky Rudd, Brett Bodine and the ageless pioneer, Dave Marcis, who recently retired after more than three decades of competition.

8. Team Chemistry

Drivers have always been the guys who are

The king of the owner/operator breed: Richard Petty.

For the less-technical drivers, taking the time to form personal relationships with their team members is an essential part of ensuring good chemistry. Their efforts must also be backed by an organization that is sensitive to the chemistry issues from top to bottom that can make or break a race team.

9. Winning with the Crew Chief

As the different jobs in the shop and garage have become more specialized, crew chiefs have taken on increased responsibility in the process of winning races. The relationship between driver and crew chief is probably the most important on-track relationship in NASCAR, and the key to that relationship is quick, effective communication. Drivers and crew chiefs must be able to give effective feedback to determine the best setup each week, and that process extends to making instantaneous calls on in-race adjustments. On an emotional level, the ability of a good driver and crew chief to balance out each other can make the difference between winning and losing during tight, tense moments when the tendency to lose control is at its highest.

10. Sponsors, Media and PR

Pleasing the sponsor has been a part of NASCAR racing from the beginning, but with the passage of time, the growing complexity of the sport has made it a much more complex task. With NASCAR sponsors expanding to include an increasing number of mainstream businesses whose products have little to do with racing or cars, pleasing the sponsor has gone well beyond the task of glad-handing, grip-and-grin photos in hospitality suites and making the occasional promotional appearance.

Drivers who succeed in this arena these days put a lot more time into the relationship—they attend meetings of the sponsor's company and

under the microscope and in the spotlight, but over time their high-income, high-profile lifestyle has created a considerable gap with the income and lifestyle of team members. Good drivers figure out a way to close that gap by finding ways to maintain team chemistry.

For "under the hood" drivers like Dale Earnhardt and Jeff Burton, who know the car inside and out, that chemistry comes with shop time, although it is possible for an overly meddlesome driver to interfere with the performance of the crew chief and the race team.

make an effort to understand the sponsor's business and the goals in sponsoring a Cup car. Such goals are often quite different for a primary sponsor and an associate sponsor, both on a business level and in terms of the personal goals of the sponsor.

Almost important as dealing with the sponsor is the ongoing task of public relations and meeting the demands of the media. This part of the driver's job has changed tremendously as well; until recently, NASCAR media coverage used to be conducted by a rather insular group that was generally considered quite driver-friendly.

With the attention the sport is receiving, though, more and more of that coverage is coming from mainstream media outlets that are far more disposed to putting drivers on the hot seat. Melting under the under the glare of the spotlight affects the perceptions of fans and sponsors, and drivers who can't control their emotions and maintain a friendly image as they handle the publicity automatically raise the bar when it comes to their required level of performance.

All of which leads to the final aspect of being a good driver: the ability to connect with the fans. In terms of off-track performance, there is no more important aspect of racing than projecting a genuine personality to the fans, and understanding that the folks who fork up the money to sit in the stands on Sunday are the root of the sport. Good drivers have the ability to get it done on the track, and before and after they find a variety of ways to sign autographs, communicate with their fan base and get across how it feels to run well, to win, or to deal with the disappointment of a tough day.

Jeff Gordon and other talented drivers know they must develop a rapport with the media—and with their fans, who fork over sizable bucks to spend Sundays (and even sunset moments) at the track.

Year	Rank	Starts	Poles	Wins
1958	37	9	0	0
1959	15	21	0	0
1960	2	40	2	3
1961	8	42	2	2
1962	2	52	4	8
1963	2	54	8	14
1964	1	61	9	9
1965	38	14	7	4
1966	3	39	16	8
1967	1	48	19	27
1968	3	49	12	16
1969	2	50	6	10
1970	4	40	9	18
1971	1	46	9	21
1972	1	31	3	8
1973	5	28	3	6
1974	1	30	7	10
1975	1	30	3	13
1976	2	30	1	3
1977	2	30	5	5
1978	6	30	0	0
1979	1	31	1	5
1980	4	31	0	2
1981	8	31	0	3
1982	5	30	0	0
1983	4	30	0	3
1984	10	30	0	2
1985	14	28	0	0
1986	14	29	0	0
1987	8	29	0	0
1988	22	29	0	0
1989	29	25	0	0
1990	26	29	0	0
1991	24	29	0	0
1992	26	29	0	0
Totals		**1184**	**126**	**200**

With President Ronald Reagan in attendance at the 1984 Firecracker 400 at Daytona, Petty won his unprecedented 200th Winston Cup race, leaving him 95 ahead of second-place David Pearson on the all-time victory list. But the final win of Petty's career was tainted—his engine failed post-race inspection—and the aftershocks of the scandal shook the Petty organization to its foundation.

WHY #1?

Seven driving championships and 200 victories are more than enough to land The King at the top. Petty put NASCAR on the map, helping to extend its boundaries beyond the South and establishing the standard for close interaction between drivers and fans.

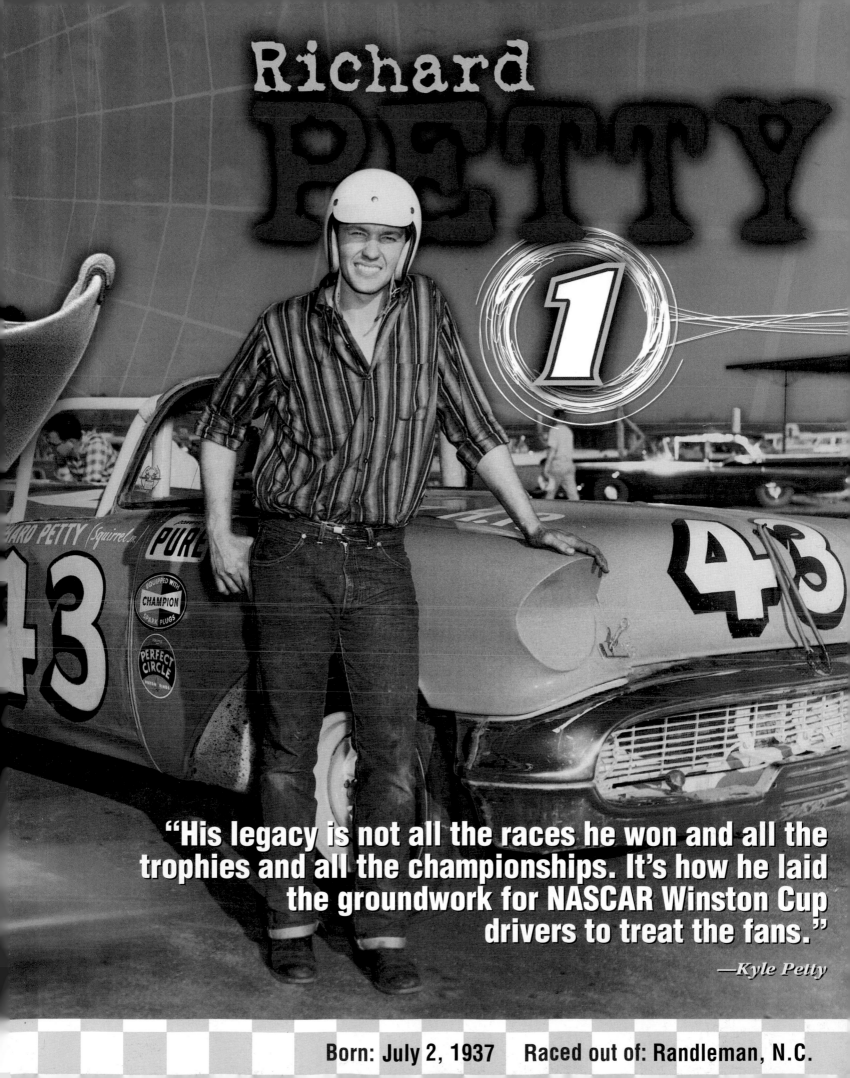

Richard PETTY

1

"His legacy is not all the races he won and all the trophies and all the championships. It's how he laid the groundwork for NASCAR Winston Cup drivers to treat the fans."

—*Kyle Petty*

Born: July 2, 1937   Raced out of: Randleman, N.C.

Dale Earnhardt

Dale EARN

2

"His desire and sheer determination to be the best at what he does is amazing. I've always thought he was the best, even when I raced against him."

—*Richard Childress*

Seven Winston Cup championships aside, it took Earnhardt 20 years to fill the most glaring hole in his resume. In 1998, after more close calls than he cared to remember, Earnhardt finally won the Daytona 500. In the process, he set a record for the world's longest receiving line, when he shook hands with virtually every crew member on pit road as he drove toward Victory Lane.

HARDT

Year	Rank	Starts	Poles	Wins
1975	NR	1	0	0
1976	103	2	0	0
1977	117	1	0	0
1978	43	5	0	0
1979	7	27	4	1
1980	1	31	0	5
1981	7	31	0	0
1982	12	30	1	1
1983	8	30	0	2
1984	4	30	0	2
1985	8	28	1	4
1986	1	29	1	5
1987	1	29	1	11
1988	3	29	0	3
1989	2	29	0	5
1990	1	29	4	9
1991	1	29	0	4
1992	12	29	1	1
1993	1	30	2	6
1994	1	31	2	4
1995	2	31	3	5
1996	4	31	2	2
1997	5	32	0	0
1998	8	33	0	1
1999	7	34	0	3
2000	2	34	0	2
2001	57	1	0	0
Totals		676	22	76

WHY #2?

The 'Intimidator' dominated from 1986-1994, getting 48 of his 76 race victories and six of his seven driving championships. No one was better at getting the most out of an ill-handling car, and his hard-charging style won him a legion of fans. He ranks second to Richard Petty because he couldn't win an unprecedented eighth title in his last six full seasons of trying.

Born: April 29, 1951   Raced out of: Kannapolis, N.C.   Died on: February 18, 2001

WHY #3?

Regarded by many as a better pure driver than Richard Petty or Dale Earnhardt, but his popularity and impact never transcended regional appeal. Pearson's 105 wins are second only to Petty's 200. True, Pearson did his damage in 574 starts, and Petty made 1,177 starts, but Pearson won only three driving titles.

A three-time Winston Cup champion who limited his racing to the superspeedways as his career drew to a close, the "Silver Fox" is perhaps best remembered not for his 105 career wins, but for his grinding crash with Richard Petty on the final lap of the 1976 Daytona 500. Petty's wrecked car came to a stop 100 feet short of the finish line, and Pearson limped home in his wounded Wood Brothers Mercury for the win.

David PEARSON

3

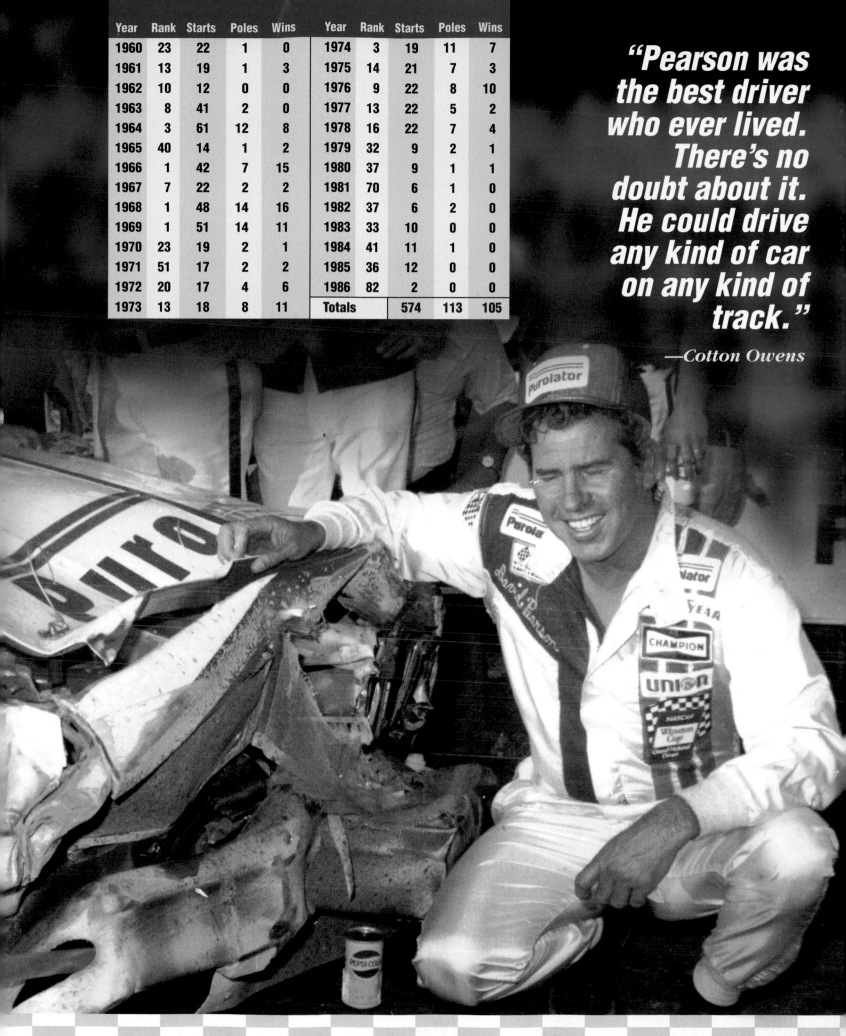

Year	Rank	Starts	Poles	Wins	Year	Rank	Starts	Poles	Wins
1960	23	22	1	0	1974	3	19	11	7
1961	13	19	1	3	1975	14	21	7	3
1962	10	12	0	0	1976	9	22	8	10
1963	8	41	2	0	1977	13	22	5	2
1964	3	61	12	8	1978	16	22	7	4
1965	40	14	1	2	1979	32	9	2	1
1966	1	42	7	15	1980	37	9	1	1
1967	7	22	2	2	1981	70	6	1	0
1968	1	48	14	16	1982	37	6	2	0
1969	1	51	14	11	1983	33	10	0	0
1970	23	19	2	1	1984	41	11	1	0
1971	51	17	2	2	1985	36	12	0	0
1972	20	17	4	6	1986	82	2	0	0
1973	13	18	8	11	Totals		574	113	105

"Pearson was the best driver who ever lived. There's no doubt about it. He could drive any kind of car on any kind of track."

—*Cotton Owens*

Born: December 12, 1934   **Raced out of: Spartanburg, S.C.**

"He's not just the driver of the future. He's the driver of the immediate future. Gordon's going to be a pain in our sides for a long time."

—*Dale Jarrett*

4
Jeff
GORDON

In 1994, "Wonder Boy" gave NASCAR fans a strong indication of what lay ahead. After winning his first Winston Cup race at Charlotte in May, Jeff won an emotionally-charged race in the inaugural Brickyard 400 at revered Indianapolis Motor Speedway in his home state. Gordon went on to win series championships in 1995, 1997, 1998 and 2001.

Year	Rank	Starts	Poles	Wins
1992	79T	1	0	0
1993	14	30	1	0
1994	8	31	1	2
1995	1	31	8	7
1996	2	31	5	10
1997	1	32	1	10
1998	1	33	7	13
1999	6	34	7	7
2000	9	34	3	3
2001	1	36	7	6
Totals		293	40	58

WHY #4?

The numbers don't lie; Gordon really is Wonder Boy. Gordon had 58 wins after 293 starts, and won his fourth driving title in 2001 at the ripe age of 30. If Gordon stays in the sport another 10 years, he'll overtake Richard Petty and Dale Earnhardt in Winston Cup titles and pass all but Petty in wins.

Born: August 4, 1971   Races out of: Pittsboro, Ind.

5 Cale YARBO

"Cale jumped in the car and pushed the throttle to the floor before he switched it on. When the green fell, he locked the throttle on 'kill', gritted his teeth, and held on."

—*Bobby Allison*

The snapshots of Yarborough's career are unforgettable—the unexpected "flight" over the first-turn wall at Darlington and the fistfight with the Allisons after the 1979 Daytona 500. But the hard charger's most significant achievement by far was winning three straight series championships (1976-78), a feat unequalled by any other driver before or since.

ROUGH

Year	Rank	Starts	Poles	Wins
1957	159	1	0	0
1959	110	1	0	0
1960	132	1	0	0
1961	NR	1	0	0
1962	50	8	0	0
1963	25	18	0	0
1964	19	24	0	0
1965	10	46	0	1
1966	18	14	0	0
1967	20	16	4	2
1968	17	21	4	6
1969	23	19	6	2
1970	34	19	5	3
1971	NR	4	0	0
1972	51	5	0	0
1973	2	28	5	4
1974	2	30	3	10
1975	9	27	3	3
1976	1	30	2	9
1977	1	30	3	9
1978	1	30	8	10
1979	4	31	1	4
1980	2	31	14	6
1981	24	18	2	2
1982	27	16	2	3
1983	28	16	3	4
1984	22	16	4	3
1985	26	16	0	2
1986	29	16	1	0
1987	29	16	0	0
1988	38	10	0	0
Totals		559	70	83

Born: March 27, 1939   Raced out of: Sardis, S.C.

Bobby
7 ALLI

Though Allison is tied for third in career wins with 84, it's not difficult to pick out the most meaningful of his victories. Allison led the final 18 laps to edge his son, the late Davey Allison, by two car lengths in the 1988 Daytona 500.

Year	Rank	Starts	Poles	Wins
1961	106	4	0	0
1965	34	8	0	0
1966	10	34	4	3
1967	4	45	2	6
1968	11	37	2	2
1969	20	27	1	5
1970	2	46	5	3
1971	4	40	8	10
1972	2	31	11	10
1973	7	27	6	2
1974	4	27	3	2
1975	24	19	3	3
1976	4	30	2	0
1977	8	30	0	0
1978	2	30	1	5
1979	3	31	3	5
1980	6	31	2	4
1981	2	31	2	5
1982	2	30	1	8
1983	1	30	0	6
1984	6	30	0	2
1985	12	28	0	0
1986	7	29	0	1
1987	9	29	1	1
1988	33	13	0	1
Totals		**717**	**57**	**84**

"If there's anybody tougher or more determined than Bobby, I've never met them."

—*Neil Bonnett*

WHY #7?

The leader of the former Alabama Gang, Allison doesn't receive as much credit as Richard Petty or David Pearson, likely because he always seemed to be on their bumpers. Allison finished second in driver points five times. A guy who did a lot with a little, he won 84 races and one points title.

SON

Not since Lee and Richard Petty finished first and second at Heidelberg Speedway in 1960 had a father and son captured the top two spots in a Winston Cup race.

Born: December 3, 1937   Raced out of: Hueytown, Ala.

8

Lee
PETTY

Only three times have a father and son finished 1-2 in a Winston Cup race. Lee Petty, a three-time series champion and the patriarch of the Petty dynasty, accomplished the feat twice. On June 14, 1959, he led son Richard—the man who would be King—to the checkered flag at Atlanta. On July 10, 1960, Lee Petty won at Pittsburgh, with Richard in the runner-up position.

"Lee was into all racing. He understood the car as well as driving. He knew you didn't have to always be the fastest to be first."

—*Tim Flock*

Year	Rank	Starts	Poles	Wins
1949	2	8	0	1
1950	3	18	0	2
1951	4	32	0	1
1952	3	32	0	3
1953	2	36	0	5
1954	1	34	3	7
1955	3	42	1	6
1956	4	47	1	2
1957	4	41	3	4
1958	1	49	4	7
1959	1	42	2	11
1960	6	39	3	5
1961	104	3	1	1
1962	73	1	0	0
1963	82	3	0	0
1964	109	2	0	0
Totals		**429**	**18**	**55**

Born: March 14, 1914   **Raced out of: Level Cross, N.C.**   **Died on: April 5, 2000**

Year	Rank	Starts	Poles	Wins
1953	NR	1	0	0
1954	55	4	1	0
1955	6	36	2	5
1956	38	13	1	0
1957	154	1	0	0
1958	8	27	0	6
1959	11	28	1	5
1960	7	34	3	3
1961	6	41	10	7
1962	20	23	2	1
1963	12	33	9	7
1964	14	29	5	3
1965	12	36	10	13
1966	49	7	3	0
Totals		**313**	**47**	**50**

9

Junior JOB

"Junior would go as hard as he could as long as he could. He would never, ever slow up no matter how far he was ahead. If the car didn't break or crash, you couldn't catch him."

—*Tim Flock*

WHY #9?

Johnson never won a driving title but gets credit for winning six championships and 140 races as a car owner. Why didn't he win a title as a driver? Simply put, Johnson drove his cars so hard that they won (50 races) or broke—there was no in between.

On Oct. 3, 1965, driving a Ford he owned, Johnson joined NASCAR's elite 50-win club with a victory at North Wilkesboro. The win would be his last as a driver, but the man who never won a Winston Cup championship behind the wheel went on to capture six titles as a car owner—three with Cale Yarborough and three with Darrell Waltrip.

Born: June 28, 1931   Raced out of: Ronda, N.C.

"He had to be good to win forty-eight races in only six years. From a winning standpoint, Herb was as fierce a competitor as anybody."

—Richard Petty

Year	Rank	Starts	Poles	Wins
1949	25	4	0	0
1950	11	13	0	1
1951	1	36	4	7
1952	2	32	10	8
1953	1	37	12	12
1954	2	34	8	12
1955	5	23	2	3
1956	3	48	2	5
1957	148	2	0	0
1962	97	1	0	0
Totals		230	38	48

10

Herb THOMAS

How good was Thomas? He won 43 races in his first 175 starts, numbers better than Jeff Gordon's. Thomas finished with 48 wins and two driving titles in only 230 starts. His career was cut short when he was seriously injured in a crash in 1956.

Herb Thomas drove the Hudson Hornet to its first series championship in 1951. Thomas finished 21st, next-to-last, in the final race of the season at Mobile, Ala., but that was all he needed to claim the first of his two titles. In his 1953 championship season, Thomas wrapped up the title with three races left on the schedule with a win at Wilson, N.C., again in a Hudson.

Born: April 6, 1923   Raced out of: Sanford, N.C.   Died on: August 9, 2000

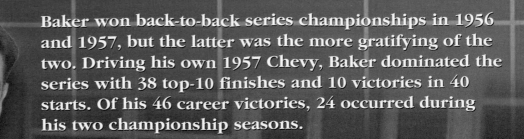

Baker won back-to-back series championships in 1956 and 1957, but the latter was the more gratifying of the two. Driving his own 1957 Chevy, Baker dominated the series with 38 top-10 finishes and 10 victories in 40 starts. Of his 46 career victories, 24 occurred during his two championship seasons.

Year	Rank	Starts	Poles	Wins
1949	48	2	0	0
1950	12	9	1	0
1951	23	11	0	0
1952	12	14	2	1
1953	4	33	4	4
1954	3	34	7	4
1955	2	42	2	3
1956	1	48	12	14
1957	1	40	6	10
1958	2	44	3	3
1959	5	35	4	1
1960	4	37	2	2
1961	10	42	1	1
1962	13	37	0	0
1963	11	47	0	1
1964	9	34	0	2
1965	17	31	0	0
1966	21	36	0	0
1967	27	21	0	0
1968	40	17	0	0
1969	NR	1	0	0
1970	NR	1	0	0
1971	NR	6	0	0
1972	NR	5	0	0
1973	101	1	0	0
1976	48	8	0	0
Totals		636	44	46

"Buck was real aggressive. He was one of those guys who didn't like running second or third. He was going to the front."

—*Cotton Owens*

WHY #11?

Baker probably has received more publicity for the driving school he started after his retirement. He was pretty good on the track, too, becoming the first driver to win consecutive championships (1956-57). He won 46 races and finished among the top five in points nine times in his career.

Buck
BAKER

11

BUCK BAKER

87 JR.

BRUSHY Mtn. MOTO

Born: March 4, 1919   Raced out of: Charlotte, N.C.

Year	Rank	Starts	Poles	Wins
1953	68	2	0	0
1954	147	2	0	0
1955	173	3	0	0
1956	166	2	0	0
1957	169	1	0	0
1959	37	17	0	2
1960	5	40	5	5
1961	1	46	4	1
1962	3	52	4	6
1963	4	53	4	8
1964	2	59	9	15
1965	1	54	9	13
1966	13	21	0	0
Totals		352	35	50

WHY #12?

Jarrett won 50 races and two driving championships—not too shabby when he retired at 35—but his greatest contribution came off the track. When NASCAR started to take off in the 1980s, Jarrett was the voice on the radio and the face on television that fans identified with.

Birthdate: October 12, 1932   Raced out of: Neton, N.C.

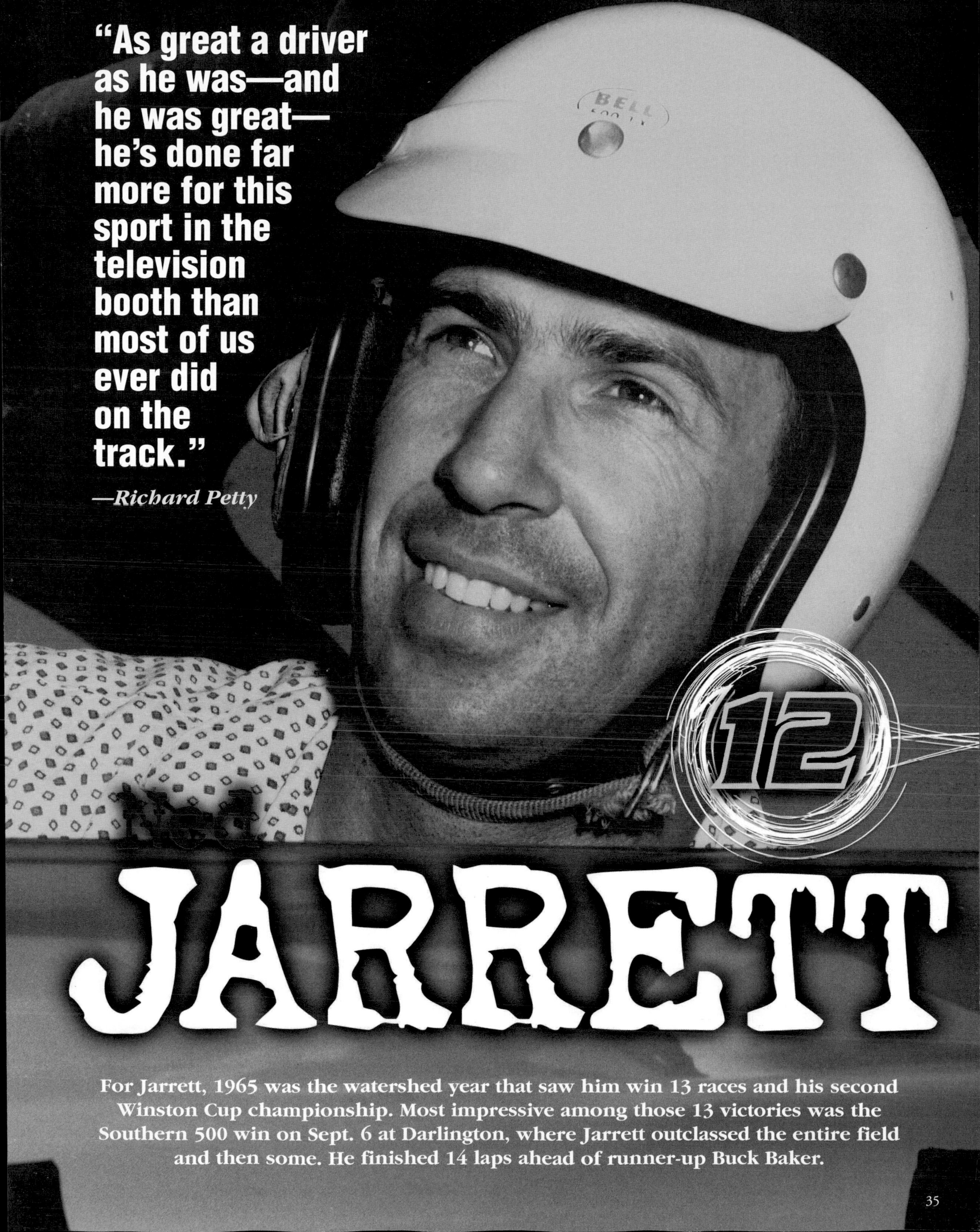

"As great a driver as he was—and he was great—he's done far more for this sport in the television booth than most of us ever did on the track."

—Richard Petty

JARRETT

12

For Jarrett, 1965 was the watershed year that saw him win 13 races and his second Winston Cup championship. Most impressive among those 13 victories was the Southern 500 win on Sept. 6 at Darlington, where Jarrett outclassed the entire field and then some. He finished 14 laps ahead of runner-up Buck Baker.

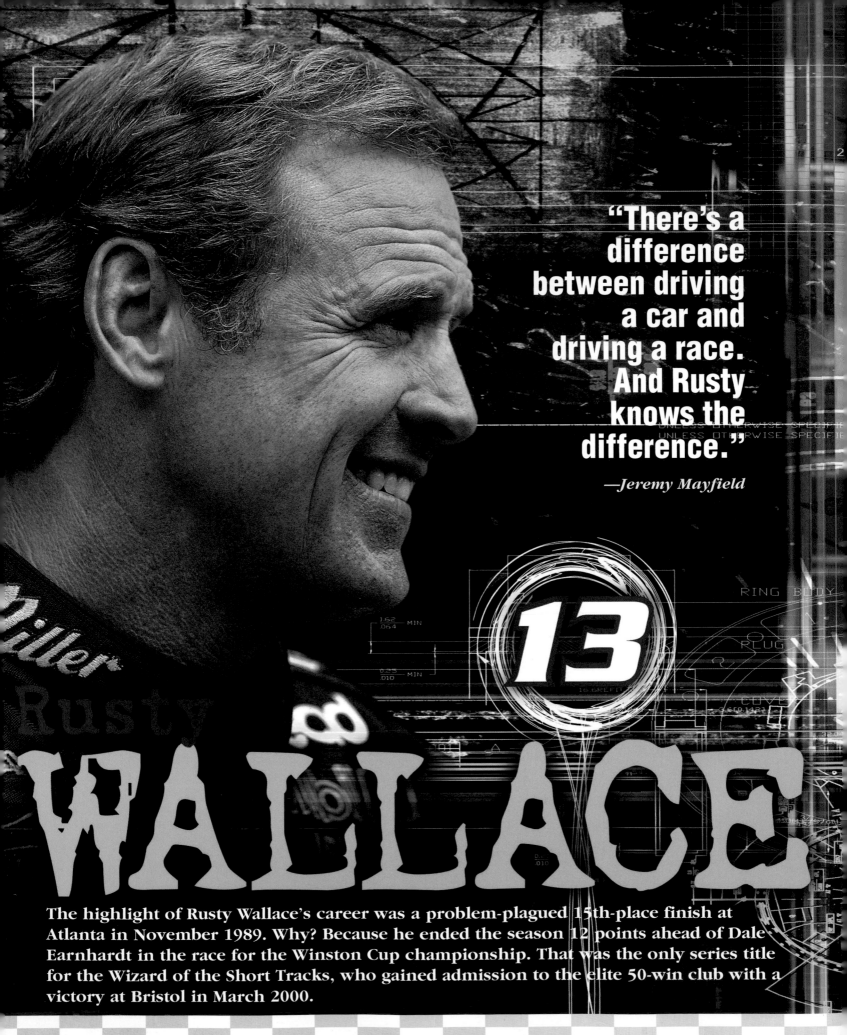

"There's a difference between driving a car and driving a race. And Rusty knows the difference."

—*Jeremy Mayfield*

13

WALLACE

The highlight of Rusty Wallace's career was a problem-plagued 15th-place finish at Atlanta in November 1989. Why? Because he ended the season 12 points ahead of Dale Earnhardt in the race for the Winston Cup championship. That was the only series title for the Wizard of the Short Tracks, who gained admission to the elite 50-win club with a victory at Bristol in March 2000.

Born: August 14, 1956 **Races out of: St. Louis, Mo.**

Year	Rank	Starts	Poles	Wins
1980	57	2	0	0
1981	64	4	0	0
1982	65	3	0	0
1984	14	30	0	0
1985	19	28	0	0
1986	6	29	0	2
1987	5	29	1	2
1988	2	29	2	6
1989	1	29	4	6
1990	6	29	2	2
1991	10	29	2	2
1992	13	29	1	1
1993	2	30	3	10
1994	3	31	2	8
1995	5	31	0	2
1996	7	31	0	5
1997	9	32	1	1
1998	4	33	4	1
1999	8	34	4	1
2000	7	34	9	4
2001	7	36	0	1
Totals		562	35	54

WHY #13?

The biggest knock on Wallace is that he hasn't won more than one championship. Yet his 54 wins rank him in the top ten of all-time. He won the driving title in 1989 and just missed out in 1988, losing to Bill Elliott by 24 points.

Fireball ROBE

14

The affable Glenn "Fireball" Roberts' most impressive victory may have come at the 1963 Southern 500, where he won a caution-free race at a then-unheard-of average speed of 129.784 m.p.h. But ironically, the lasting memory from Roberts' illustrious career is that of the fiery crash that claimed his life. Badly burned in the World 600 at Charlotte on May 24, 1964, Roberts succumbed to his injuries on July 2.

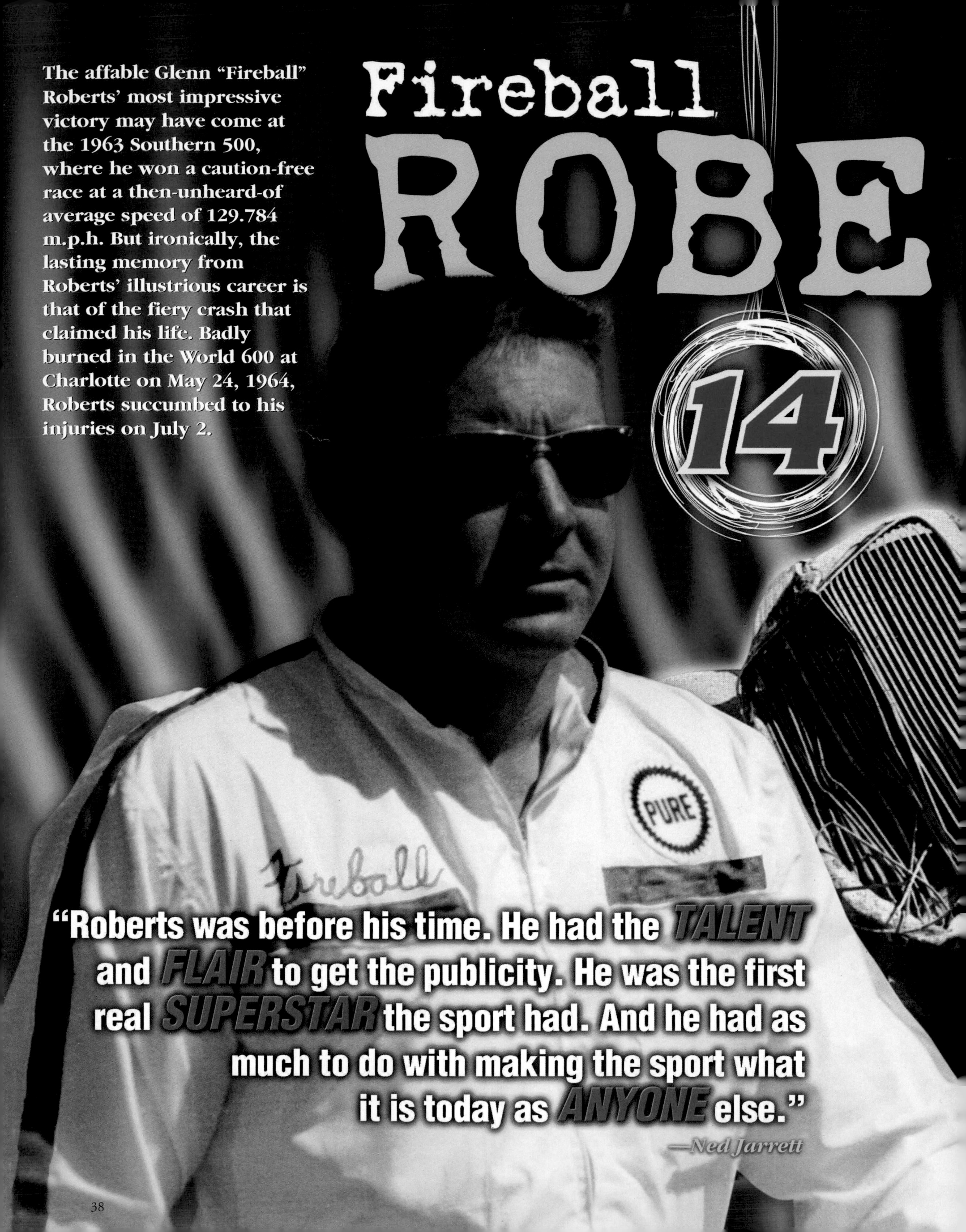

PURE

Fireball

"Roberts was before his time. He had the *TALENT* and *FLAIR* to get the publicity. He was the first real *SUPERSTAR* the sport had. And he had as much to do with making the sport what it is today as *ANYONE* else."

—*Ned Jarrett*

RTS

Year	Rank	Starts	Poles	Wins
1950	2	9	1	1
1951	12	9	0	0
1952	59	7	0	0
1953	132	2	0	0
1954	22	5	0	0
1955	201	2	1	0
1956	7	33	3	5
1957	6	42	4	8
1958	11	10	0	5
1959	16	8	3	1
1960	29	9	6	2
1961	5	22	6	2
1962	8	19	9	3
1963	5	20	2	4
1964	27	9	0	1
Totals		231	35	33

Born: January 20, 1935   Raced out of: Daytona Beach, Fla.   Died on: July 2, 1964

"Awesome Bill from Dawsonville" earned another nickname for his victory in the 1985 Southern 500. In a season that saw him win 11 races and 11 poles, Elliott was the first driver to collect a $1-million bonus for winning a designated race (the Winston Million offered by R.J. Reynolds Tobacco Co.). About the only thing "Million Dollar Bill" didn't win in 1985 was the series championship—he finished second to Darrell Waltrip.

"As far as I'm concerned, 'Bill Elliott' is just another way of saying fast."

—Harry Melling

WHY #15?

Awesome Bill from Dawsonville brought new meaning to the word speed, pushing beyond 212 mph in qualifying before restrictor plates. His impact on the sport? He has only one driving title and one victory since 1994, but fans voted him most popular driver 15 of the past 18 years. Fireball edges Elliott with a better nickname.

Born: October 8, 1955   Races out of: Dawsonville, Ga.

Year	Rank	Starts	Poles	Wins
1976	41	7	0	0
1977	35	10	0	0
1978	33	10	0	0
1979	28	14	0	0
1980	34	11	0	0
1981	30	13	1	0
1982	25	21	1	0
1983	3	30	0	1
1984	3	30	4	3
1985	2	28	11	11
1986	4	29	4	2
1987	2	29	8	6
1988	1	29	6	6
1989	6	29	2	3
1990	4	29	2	1
1991	11	29	2	1
1992	2	29	2	5
1993	8	30	2	0
1994	10	31	1	1
1995	8	31	2	0
1996	30	24	0	0
1997	8	32	1	0
1998	18	32	0	0
1999	21	34	0	0
2000	21	32	0	0
2001	15	36	2	1
Totals		659	51	41

Bill
ELLIOTT

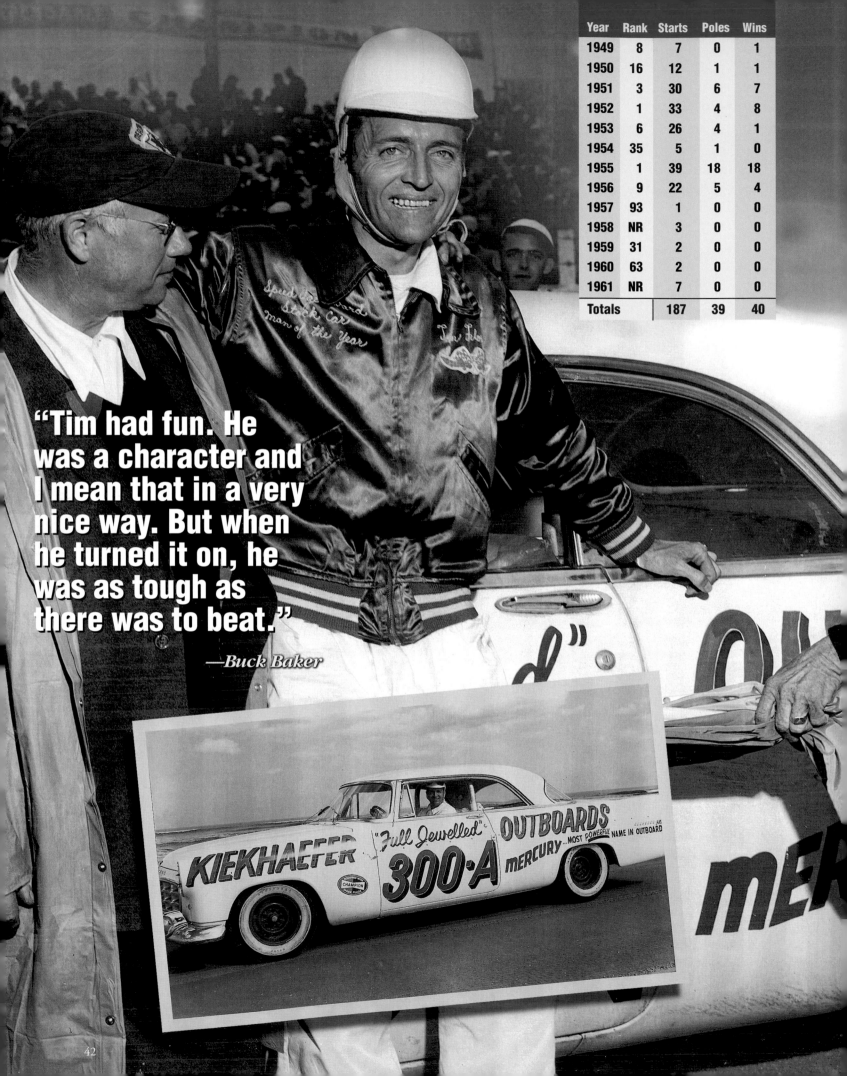

Year	Rank	Starts	Poles	Wins
1949	8	7	0	1
1950	16	12	1	1
1951	3	30	6	7
1952	1	33	4	8
1953	6	26	4	1
1954	35	5	1	0
1955	1	39	18	18
1956	9	22	5	4
1957	93	1	0	0
1958	NR	3	0	0
1959	31	2	0	0
1960	63	2	0	0
1961	NR	7	0	0
Totals		**187**	**39**	**40**

"Tim had fun. He was a character and I mean that in a very nice way. But when he turned it on, he was as tough as there was to beat."

—*Buck Baker*

WHY #16?

Flock finished with 40 wins, the same as Bill Elliott, but his two driving titles aren't enough to weigh more than Elliott's impact on the sport. Flock, whose father was a tightrope walker, scores points because he raced eight times with his pet monkey in the co-pilot's seat.

16

Tim FLOCK

The most successful of the three racing Flock brothers (Tim, Fonty and Bob) won the first of his two series championships in 1952, driving a Hudson owned by Ted Chester. Flock won the title despite flipping his car and finishing 12th in the final race of the season at Palm Beach Speedway. "I bet I'm the only driver who has won the championship on his head," Flock said after the race.

Born: May 11, 1924   **Raced out of: Atlanta, Ga.**   **Died on: March 31, 1998**

Year	Rank	Starts	Poles	Wins
1961	158T	1	0	0
1963	28	27	0	0
1964	18	19	0	1
1965	75	4	1	0
1966	53	9	0	0
1967	14	12	0	0
1968	2	49	3	3
1969	6	50	20	17
1970	1	47	13	11
1971	23	25	5	4
1972	19	27	8	1
1973	26	19	0	0
1974	33	11	0	0
1975	48	6	0	0
1976	114	2	0	0
Totals		308	50	37

Bobby Isaac had his day in the sun in 1970, when he won 11 races and his only Winston Cup championship. With points leader Richard Petty on the sidelines due to injuries suffered in a crash at Darlington a week earlier, Isaac won the "Beltsville (Md.) 300" to take over first place in the standings. He secured the championship with a seventh-place finish at Rockingham in the next-to-last race of the year.

17
Bobby
ISAAC

"Bobby Isaac was flat-out fast."

—Cale Yarborough

Born: August 1, 1932   **Raced out of: Catawba, N.C.**   **Died on: August 14, 1977**

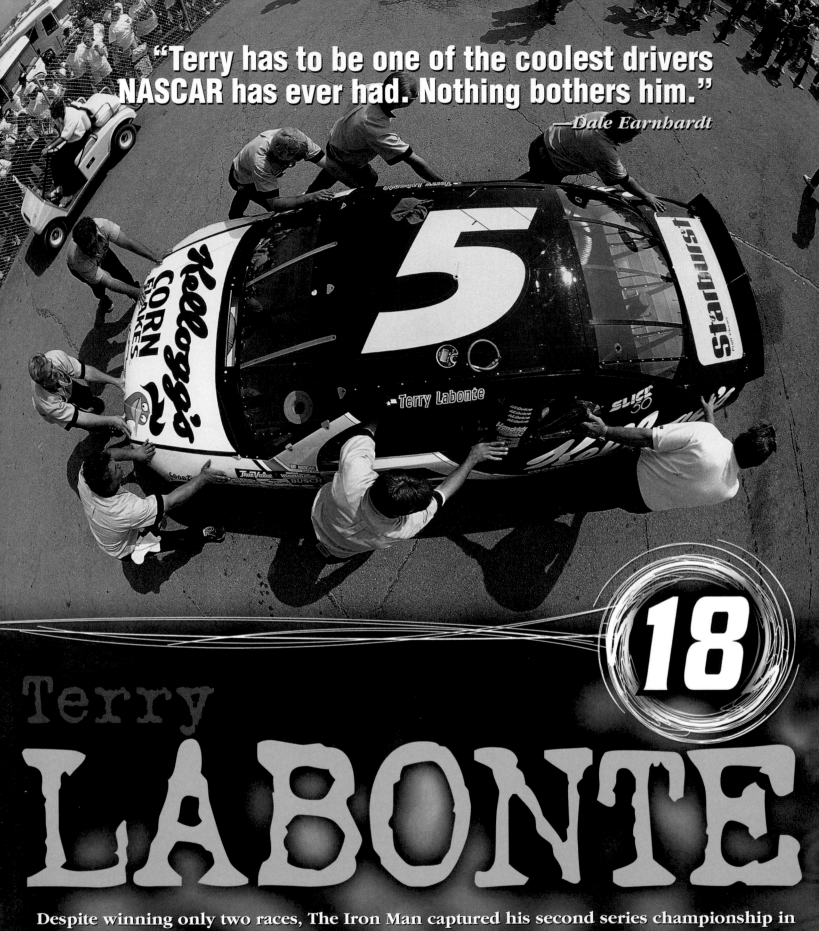

"Terry has to be one of the coolest drivers NASCAR has ever had. Nothing bothers him."
—Dale Earnhardt

18

Terry LABONTE

Despite winning only two races, The Iron Man captured his second series championship in 1996. Labonte locked up the title with a fifth-place finish at Atlanta in November—in a race won by his brother Bobby. Injuries suffered in a crash at the 2000 Pepsi 400 at Daytona ended Terry's series-record streak of 655 consecutive starts.

Born: November 16, 1956   Races out of: Corpus Christi, Texas

Year	Rank	Starts	Poles	Wins
1978	39	5	0	0
1979	10	31	0	0
1980	8	31	0	1
1981	4	31	2	0
1982	3	30	2	0
1983	5	30	3	1
1984	1	30	2	2
1985	7	28	4	1
1986	12	29	1	1
1987	3	29	4	1
1988	4	29	1	1
1989	10	29	0	2
1990	15	29	0	0
1991	18	29	1	0
1992	8	29	0	0
1993	18	30	0	0
1994	7	31	0	3
1995	6	31	1	3
1996	1	31	4	2
1997	6	32	0	1
1998	9	33	0	1
1999	12	34	0	1
2000	17	32	1	0
2001	23	36	0	0
Totals		**709**	**26**	**21**

WHY #18?

Why isn't Labonte, with two driving championships to his credit, higher on the list? Because he won only two races each of those seasons. With over 700 starts, a record 655 in a row, he has only 21 wins—not bad, but numbers that would put him much lower had he not won the two titles.

47

WHY #19?

With two driving titles and 24 wins—three more than Terry Labonte—why is Weatherly ranked lower? Two reasons: Labonte gets points for his ironman streak and still might win a race or two before he's done. Weatherly won back-to-back titles in 1962 and 1963; he died in 1964 from injuries in a race.

"Joe was one of the pioneers in helping to develop automobile racing. Plus, he was one great racer."

—*track owner Paul Sawyer*

19

Joe WEA

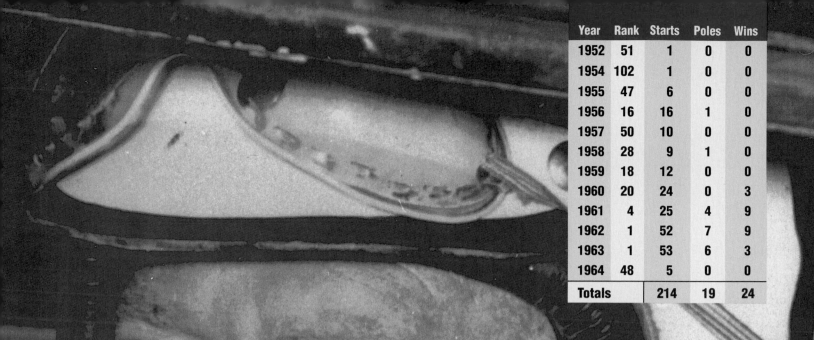

Year	Rank	Starts	Poles	Wins
1952	51	1	0	0
1954	102	1	0	0
1955	47	6	0	0
1956	16	16	1	0
1957	50	10	0	0
1958	28	9	1	0
1959	18	12	0	0
1960	20	24	0	3
1961	4	25	4	9
1962	1	52	7	9
1963	1	53	6	3
1964	48	5	0	0
Totals		214	19	24

THERLY

On Oct. 14, 1962, in the National 400 at Charlotte Motor Speedway, Weatherly clinched the first of his back-to-back series championships with a fifth-place finish in his No. 8 Pontiac. Significantly, it was the first and only title for car owner Bud Moore, who nevertheless would become one of the most influential figures in NASCAR racing.

Born: May 29, 1922   **Raced out of: Norfolk, Va.**   **Died on: January 19, 1964**

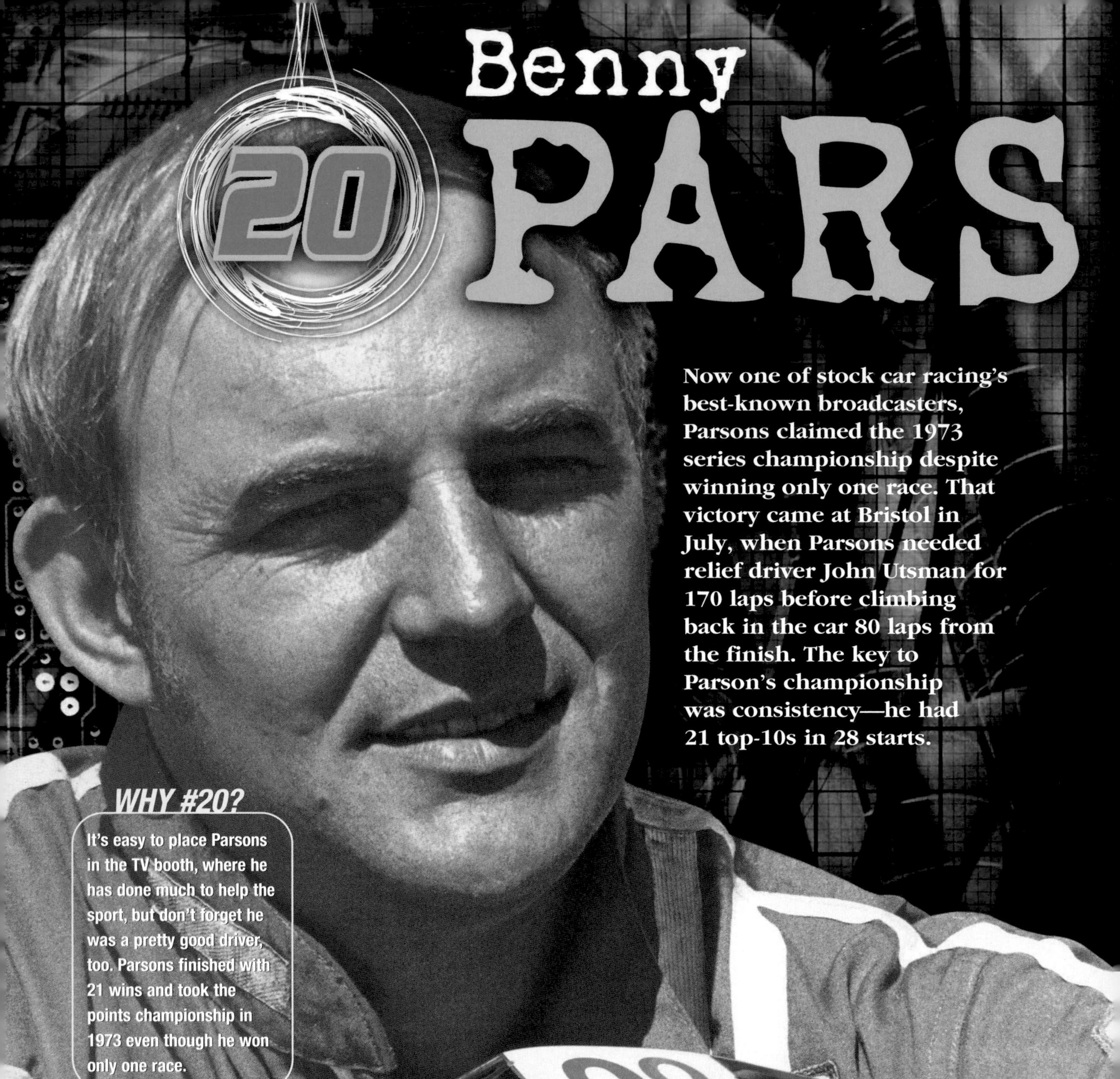

Benny
PARS

20

Now one of stock car racing's best-known broadcasters, Parsons claimed the 1973 series championship despite winning only one race. That victory came at Bristol in July, when Parsons needed relief driver John Utsman for 170 laps before climbing back in the car 80 laps from the finish. The key to Parson's championship was consistency—he had 21 top-10s in 28 starts.

WHY #20?

It's easy to place Parsons in the TV booth, where he has done much to help the sport, but don't forget he was a pretty good driver, too. Parsons finished with 21 wins and took the points championship in 1973 even though he won only one race.

427 C.I.

427 C.I.

76

98

Benny PARSON

TORINO Cobra

98

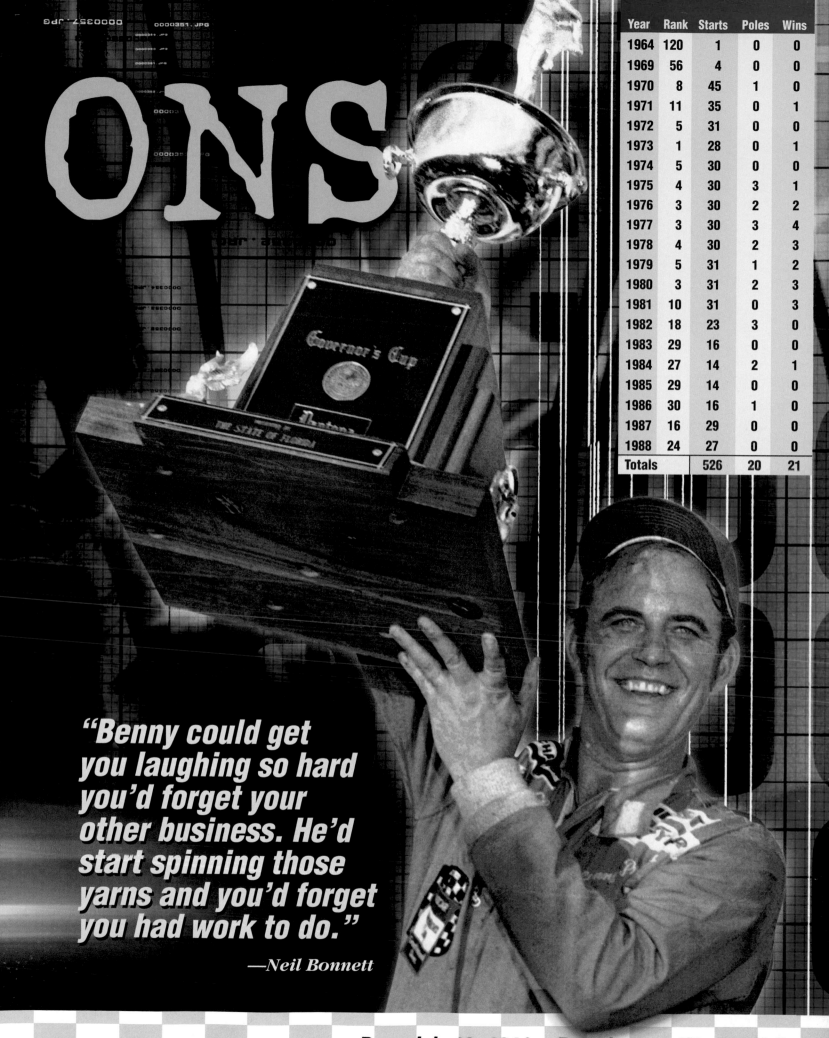

ONS

Year	Rank	Starts	Poles	Wins
1964	120	1	0	0
1969	56	4	0	0
1970	8	45	1	0
1971	11	35	0	1
1972	5	31	0	0
1973	1	28	0	1
1974	5	30	0	0
1975	4	30	3	1
1976	3	30	2	2
1977	3	30	3	4
1978	4	30	2	3
1979	5	31	1	2
1980	3	31	2	3
1981	10	31	0	3
1982	18	23	3	0
1983	29	16	0	0
1984	27	14	2	1
1985	29	14	0	0
1986	30	16	1	0
1987	16	29	0	0
1988	24	27	0	0
Totals		526	20	21

"Benny could get you laughing so hard you'd forget your other business. He'd start spinning those yarns and you'd forget you had work to do."

—*Neil Bonnett*

Born: July 12, 1941   **Raced out of: Ellerbe, N.C.**

Year	Rank	Starts	Poles	Wins
1984	85	3	0	0
1986	107T	1	0	0
1987	26	24	0	0
1988	23	29	0	0
1989	24	29	0	0
1990	25	24	0	0
1991	17	29	0	1
1992	19	29	0	0
1993	4	30	0	1
1994	16	30	0	1
1995	13	31	1	1
1996	3	31	2	4
1997	2	32	2	7
1998	3	33	2	3
1999	1	34	0	4
2000	4	34	3	2
2001	5	36	5	4
Totals		459	15	28

"It's very rare that you get a driver who is fast and *SMOOTH* and still a perfectionist."

—Robert Yates

Born: November 26, 1956   Races out of: Hickory, N.C.

21

Dale JARRETT

Though Jarrett won the 1999 Winston Cup title in convincing fashion in Robert Yates' No. 88 Ford, the highlight of his career came much earlier, in the 1993 Daytona 500. With his father, Ned Jarrett, barely able to contain himself in the broadcast booth, Jarrett beat Dale Earnhardt to the finish line to win the Super Bowl of Stock Car racing.

53

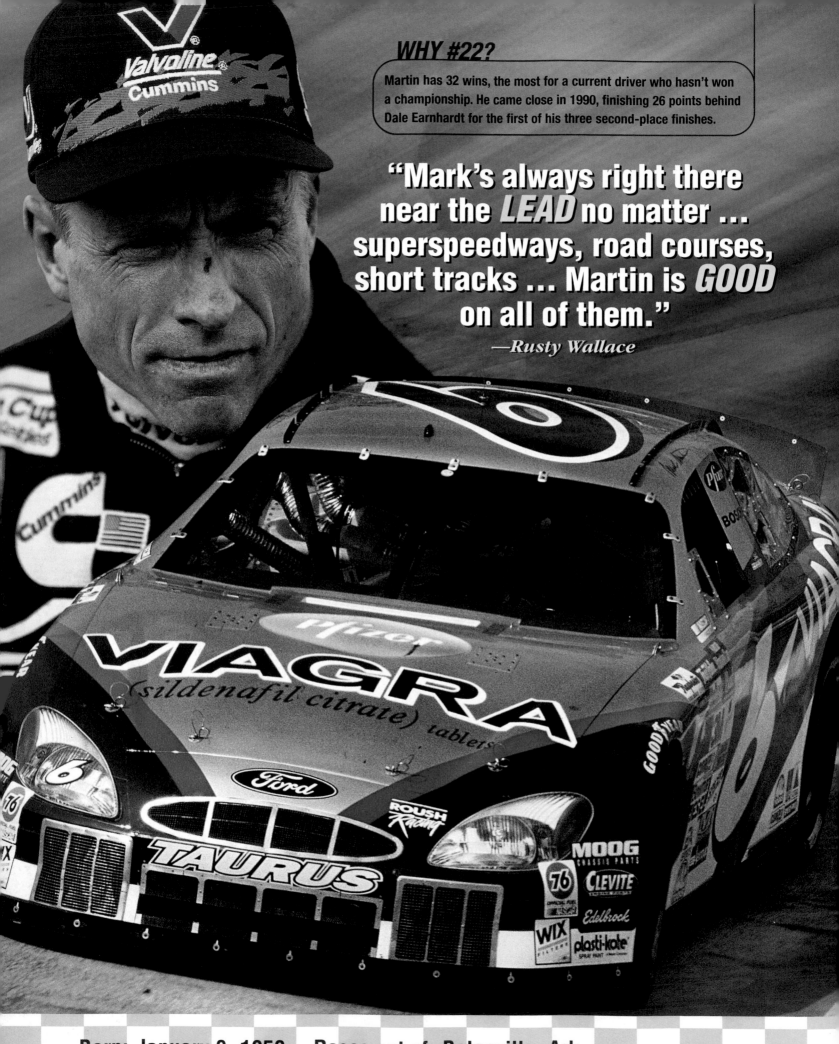

"Mark's always right there near the *LEAD* no matter … superspeedways, road courses, short tracks … Martin is *GOOD* on all of them."

—*Rusty Wallace*

Born: January 9, 1959   Races out of: Batesville, Ark.

The most pivotal moment in Mark Martin's career did not involve his modern-day-record-tying four straight wins in 1993 or his record number of victories in the Busch Series. On Feb. 25, 1990 at Richmond, Martin lost 46 championship points, and his Roush Racing team drew a $40,000 fine for a carburetor infraction discovered after Martin won the race. Martin lost the 1990 series title to Dale Earnhardt by 26 points.

Mark MARTIN

Year	Rank	Starts	Poles	Wins
1981	42	5	2	0
1982	14	30	0	0
1983	30	16	0	0
1986	48	5	0	0
1987	101T	1	0	0
1988	15	29	1	0
1989	3	29	6	1
1990	2	29	3	3
1991	6	29	5	1
1992	6	29	1	2
1993	3	30	5	5
1994	2	31	1	2
1995	4	31	4	4
1996	5	31	4	0
1997	3	32	3	4
1998	2	33	3	7
1999	3	34	1	2
2000	8	34	0	1
2001	12	36	2	0
Totals		494	41	32

"Rex was real smooth. When you were racing Rex for the win, you couldn't relax until the checkered flag fell. He was very tenacious."

—*Ned Jarrett*

WHY #23?

All but one of his 26 wins came on short tracks. White, who won one points championship, was known for his consistency—he finished in the top five in 110 of his 233 races.

Year	Rank	Starts	Poles	Wins
1956	11	24	1	0
1957	21	9	1	0
1958	7	22	7	2
1959	10	19	4	3
1960	1	40	3	6
1961	2	47	7	7
1962	5	37	9	8
1963	9	25	3	0
1964	28	6	0	0
Totals		**229**	**35**	**26**

"Little Rex" brought Chevrolet its second series championship in 1960, and he did so with 35 top-10 finishes and six victories in 40 starts. One of the most memorable races of the 1960 season was White's victory over Joe Weatherly in the Old Dominion 500 at Martinsville. The 5-foot-4, 145-pound White edged Weatherly by one car length.

Rex WHITE

23

BOONVILLE, N.C.

N.C. **9**

BUILT BY
STEELMAN
MOTOR
CO.

Born: August 17, 1929   Raced out of: Spartanburg, S.C.

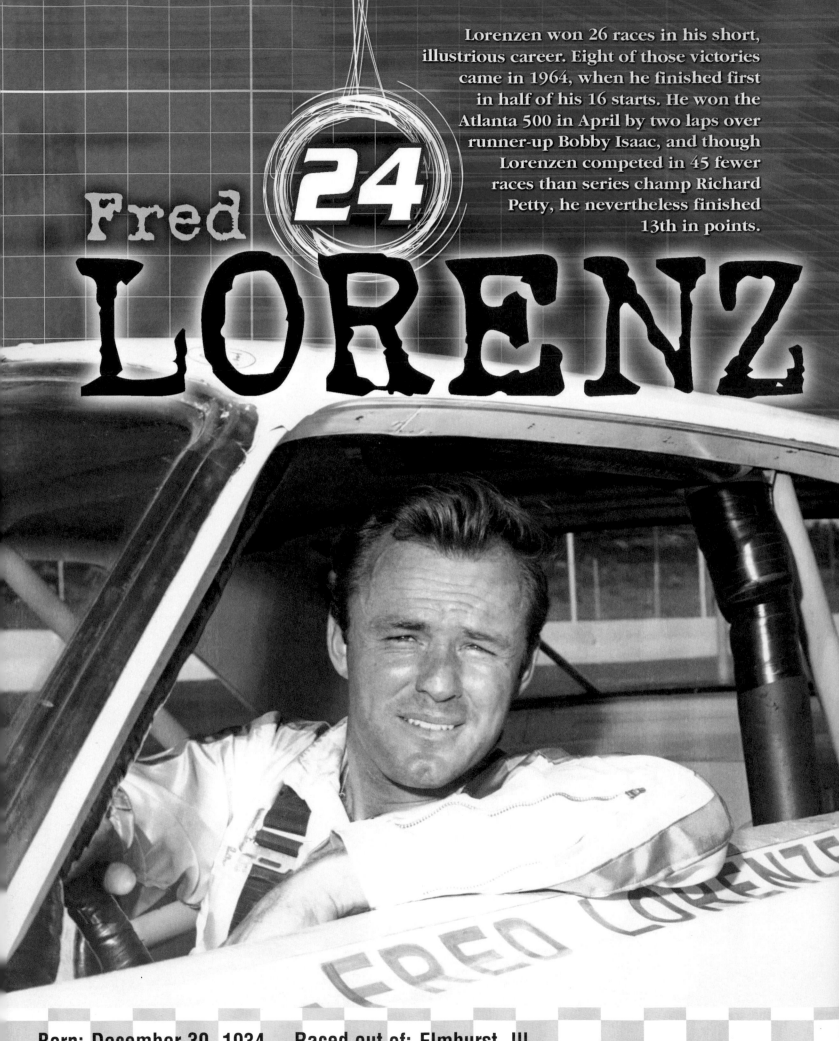

Lorenzen won 26 races in his short, illustrious career. Eight of those victories came in 1964, when he finished first in half of his 16 starts. He won the Atlanta 500 in April by two laps over runner-up Bobby Isaac, and though Lorenzen competed in 45 fewer races than series champ Richard Petty, he nevertheless finished 13th in points.

24

Fred LORENZ

Born: December 30, 1934   **Raced out of: Elmhurst, Ill.**

"I always thought he quit in his prime. Had Fred continued to race, he might have been high on the all-time list."

—*Richard Petty*

Year	Rank	Starts	Poles	Wins
1956	120	7	0	0
1960	15	10	0	0
1961	19	15	4	3
1962	7	19	3	2
1963	3	29	9	6
1964	13	16	7	8
1965	13	17	6	4
1966	23	11	2	2
1967	29	5	0	1
1970	54	7	1	0
1971	45	14	1	0
1972	39	8	0	0
Totals		**158**	**33**	**26**

WHY #24?

Fast Freddie won 26 races from 1961-67, then unexpectedly retired. He came back in 1970 but ran only 29 more races before retiring. A guy who later said he quit too soon, Lorenzen had 75 top-five finishes in 158 starts.

"Davey Allison was a special talent; a great

WHY #25?

It's natural to wonder how many races and championships Allison might have won had he not died after a helicopter crash in 1993. He won 19 times in 191 starts. He won five races in 1991 and 1992 and finished third in points both seasons.

Year	Rank	Starts	Poles	Wins
1985	71	3	0	0
1986	47	5	0	0
1987	21	22	5	2
1988	8	29	3	2
1989	11	29	1	2
1990	13	29	0	2
1991	3	29	3	5
1992	3	29	2	5
1993	31	16	0	1
Totals		191	14	19

Havoline

Davey

ALLI

driver on the track, a quality person off the track."

—Robert Yates

The son of former champion Bobby Allison, Davey appeared headed for a title of his own when he assumed the points lead with a dramatic victory in the Pyroil 500K at Phoenix on Nov. 1, 1992. Allison needed a fifth-place finish the following week at Atlanta to claim the championship, but his title hopes were dashed in a collision with Ernie Irvan late in the race. Less than a year later, a helicopter crash at Talladega would claim Allison's life.

Born: February 25, 1961   Raced out of: Hueytown, Ala.   Died on: July 13, 1993

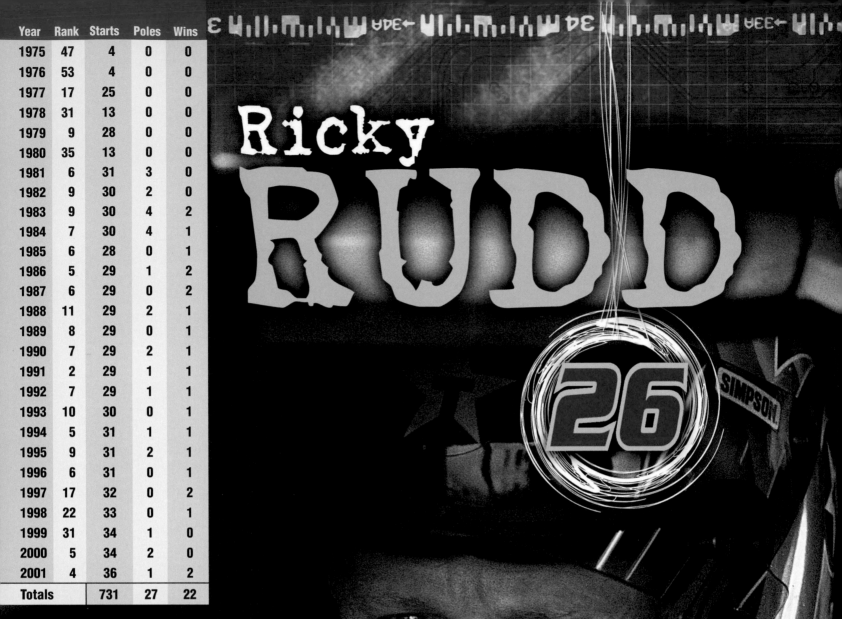

Year	Rank	Starts	Poles	Wins
1975	47	4	0	0
1976	53	4	0	0
1977	17	25	0	0
1978	31	13	0	0
1979	9	28	0	0
1980	35	13	0	0
1981	6	31	3	0
1982	9	30	2	0
1983	9	30	4	2
1984	7	30	4	1
1985	6	28	0	1
1986	5	29	1	2
1987	6	29	0	2
1988	11	29	2	1
1989	8	29	0	1
1990	7	29	2	1
1991	2	29	1	1
1992	7	29	1	1
1993	10	30	0	1
1994	5	31	1	1
1995	9	31	2	1
1996	6	31	0	1
1997	17	32	0	2
1998	22	33	0	1
1999	31	34	1	0
2000	5	34	2	0
2001	4	36	1	2
Totals		**731**	**27**	**22**

Ricky RUDD

26

"Ricky was the most pleasant driver we ever worked with. He did a fine job for us. He knew what it took to win races, which is what I think has made him a successful driver."

—*car owner Bud Moore*

Born: September 12, 1956   Races out of: Chesapeake, Va.

In his penultimate season as an owner/driver, Rudd extended his series-best winning streak to 16 years—and he did it the hard way. At Martinsville in September of 1998, Rudd had the "hottest" car on the track in more ways than one. Despite suffering painful burns and blisters, he took the checkered flag, and the win gave him at least one victory per season (and never more than two) for 16 straight years. The streak ended in 1999.

WHY #26?

Rudd has been driving Winston Cup cars since 1975 but never has won a championship. Rudd's revival in 2001—finishing fourth in points—proves he still has something left.

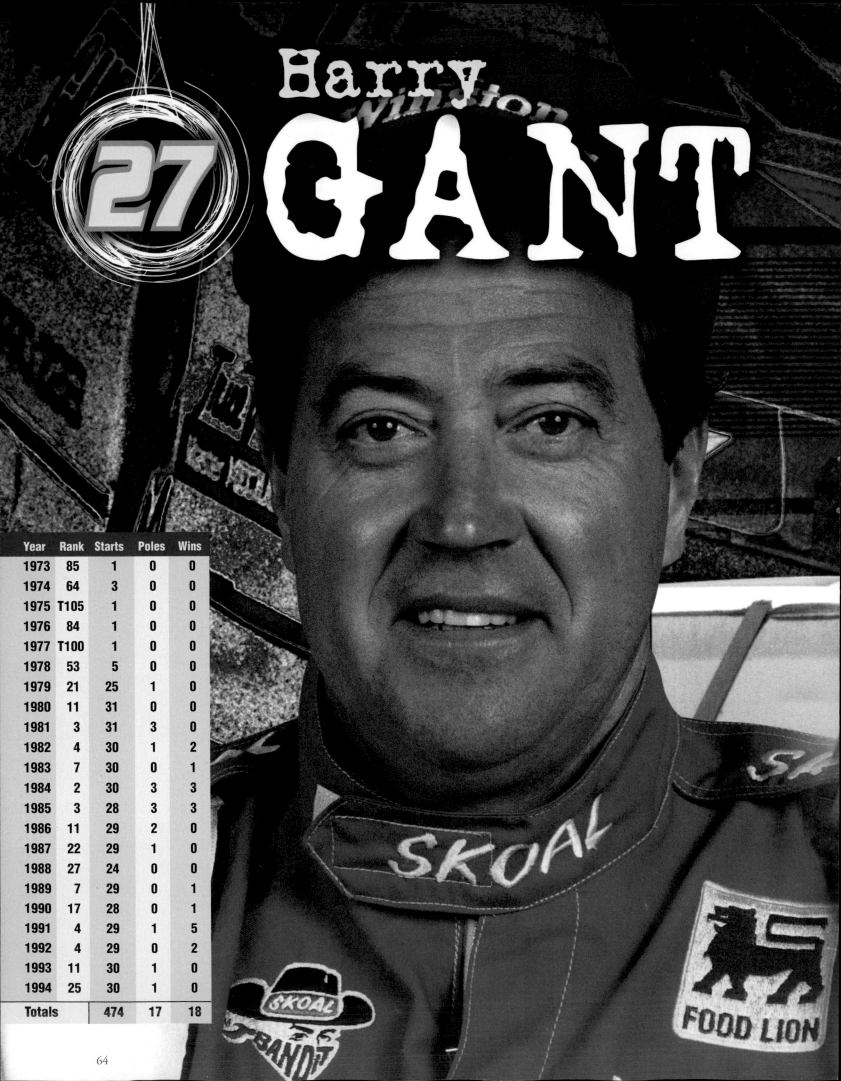

Harry GANT

27

Year	Rank	Starts	Poles	Wins
1973	85	1	0	0
1974	64	3	0	0
1975	T105	1	0	0
1976	84	1	0	0
1977	T100	1	0	0
1978	53	5	0	0
1979	21	25	1	0
1980	11	31	0	0
1981	3	31	3	0
1982	4	30	1	2
1983	7	30	0	1
1984	2	30	3	3
1985	3	28	3	3
1986	11	29	2	0
1987	22	29	1	0
1988	27	24	0	0
1989	7	29	0	1
1990	17	28	0	1
1991	4	29	1	5
1992	4	29	0	2
1993	11	30	1	0
1994	25	30	1	0
Totals		474	17	18

If baseball star Reggie Jackson will forever be remembered as Mr. October for his World Series heroics, Gant will never surrender his designation as racing's Mr. September. Starting with the Southern 500 on Sept. 1, 1991, Handsome Harry won consecutive races at Darlington, Richmond, Dover and Martinsville. On Sept. 29 at North Wilkesboro, he narrowly missed an unprecedented fifth straight modern-era victory when he finished second—1.47 seconds behind Dale Earnhardt.

WHY #27?

Handsome Harry was 39 in his rookie season in Winston Cup racing. Still, he won 18 races in his career and is the oldest driver to win a Cup race. He was 52 when he won at Michigan, his last victory, in 1992.

"Harry was one driver that other drivers pulled for. There was never a sad face when Harry won."

—Terry Labonte

Born: January 10, 1940   Raced out of: Taylorsville, N.C.

Controversial for his activities off the track as the first president of Charlotte Motor Speedway and an unsuccessful union organizer, Turner nevertheless won 17 races during a career that was interrupted by a four-year suspension from 1961 to 1965. NASCAR banned Turner because of his organizing activities under the auspices of the Teamsters. The most fulfilling victory of his career was his win over Cale Yarborough in the American 500 at Rockingham —Turner's first triumph after the lifting of his suspension.

Curtis TURNER

28

Year	Rank	Starts	Poles	Wins
1949	6	6	1	1
1950	5	16	4	4
1951	NR	12	0	3
1952	50	7	0	0
1953	10	19	3	1
1954	9	10	1	1
1955	34	9	0	0
1956	20	13	0	1
1957	22	10	1	0
1958	20	17	1	3
1959	24	10	1	2
1960	36	9	1	0
1961	NR	8	0	0
1965	39	7	0	1
1966	24	21	2	0
1967	71	4	2	0
1968	47	6	0	0
Totals		184	17	17

WHY #28?

The Blond Blizzard was regarded by many as the best driver in the 1950s. He finished with 17 wins. A businessman who worked in lumber and real estate, he helped build Charlotte Motor Speedway.

"Curtis Turner was the greatest race driver I have ever seen."

—*Junior Johnson*

DRIVEN BY BILL FRANCE CURTIS TURNER

OFFICIAL "NASCAR" PACE CAR

Born: April 12, 1924   Raced out of: Roanoke, Va.   Died on: October 4, 1970

29

Despite his 25 Winston Cup victories, Paschal may have seemed a lesser light in the stock car racing firmament because of the quality of his competition—most notably teammate Richard Petty. Twice within a three-week period in 1962, however, Paschal outshone the King. On Nov. 4, 1962, he and Petty finished 1-2 at Birmingham; 18 days later, on Thanksgiving Day, Paschal won the Turkey Day 200 at Tar Heel Speedway in Randleman, N.C.—Petty's home turf.

Jim PASCH

AL

Year	Rank	Starts	Poles	Wins
1949	NR	1	0	0
1950	24	6	0	0
1951	15	16	0	0
1952	18	15	0	0
1953	7	24	1	1
1954	7	27	2	1
1955	8	36	2	3
1956	5	42	1	1
1957	10	35	0	0
1958	42	6	1	1
1959	25	6	0	0
1960	9	10	0	0
1961	9	23	1	2
1962	6	39	0	4
1963	19	32	1	5
1964	7	22	0	1
1965	35	10	0	0
1966	14	18	2	2
1967	6	45	1	4
1968	104	1	0	0
1970	NR	1	0	0
1971	NR	6	0	0
1972	NR	1	0	0
Totals		**422**	**12**	**25**

Born: December 5, 1926   Raced out of: High Point, N.C.

"He's quite a competitor. He's very, very intense, a lot like my dad."

—*Terry Labonte*

WHY #30?

It's likely that Labonte will pass brother Terry in wins and championships before he hangs up his helmet. Bobby won the points title in 2000; he is with a team that gives him a chance to win every week.

Year	Rank	Starts	Poles	Wins
1991	66	2	0	0
1993	19	30	1	0
1994	21	31	0	0
1995	10	31	2	3
1996	11	31	4	1
1997	7	32	3	1
1998	6	33	3	2
1999	2	34	5	5
2000	1	34	2	4
2001	6	36	1	2
Totals		294	21	18

In 2000, Labonte captured the Winston Cup championship in convincing fashion—joining brother Terry as the only pair of siblings ever to win the title. Bobby finished every race in 2000 and completed a remarkable 10,158 laps of a possible 10,167. He won four races, none more important to his championship run than the Pepsi 400 at Daytona, where he was first off pit road just before a rainstorm and won the event without leading a green-flag lap.

30

Bobby LABONTE

Born: May 8, 1964   Races out of: Corpus Christi, Texas

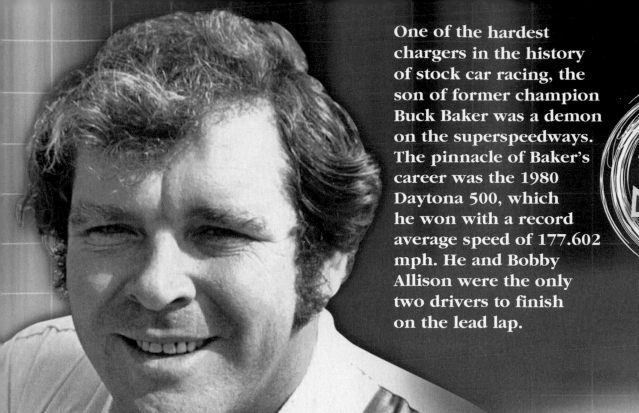

One of the hardest chargers in the history of stock car racing, the son of former champion Buck Baker was a demon on the superspeedways. The pinnacle of Baker's career was the 1980 Daytona 500, which he won with a record average speed of 177.602 mph. He and Bobby Allison were the only two drivers to finish on the lead lap.

31

Year	Rank	Starts	Poles	Wins	Year	Rank	Starts	Poles	Wins
1959	26	12	0	0	1976	7	30	2	1
1960	38	15	0	0	1977	5	30	0	0
1961	31	14	0	0	1978	24	19	1	0
1962	23	31	0	0	1979	15	26	7	3
1963	52	8	0	0	1980	21	19	6	2
1964	31	33	0	0	1981	27	16	0	0
1965	9	42	0	0	1982	23	23	1	0
1966	22	41	1	0	1983	21	21	1	1
1967	15	20	0	1	1984	21	21	1	0
1968	13	38	4	1	1985	17	28	0	0
1969	22	18	3	0	1986	24	17	0	0
1970	24	18	1	1	1987	24	20	0	0
1971	15	19	1	1	1988	29	17	0	0
1972	24	17	1	2	1990	41	8	0	0
1973	6	27	5	2	1991	40	6	0	0
1974	7	19	2	0	1992	48	3	0	0
1975	15	23	3	4	**Totals**		**699**	**40**	**19**

WHY #31?

Bigfoot liked to go fast and liked the big tracks—Daytona and Talladega. Baker was the first Winston Cup driver to run a lap of 200 mph during an in-season test in 1970 at Talladega. He finished with 19 wins before moving to the broadcast booth.

Buddy
BAKER

"When Buddy was hooked up on a super-speedway, it was almost impossible to hold onto him."

—Darrell Waltrip

TONA

88 Charger 88

Born: January 5, 1941   **Raced out of: Charlotte, N.C.**

LeeRoy YARBRO

32

He overcame a myriad of personal problems to win 14 Winston Cup races. Yarbrough enjoyed his most successful season in 1969, when he won seven races. Included in that total was a dramatic victory in the Daytona 500, where Yarbrough passed Chargin' Charlie Glotzbach on the final lap to win by a car length.

Year	Rank	Starts	Poles	Wins
1960	137	1	0	0
1962	36	12	0	0
1963	26	14	1	0
1964	15	34	0	2
1965	37	14	0	0
1966	26	9	2	1
1967	37	15	0	1
1968	16	26	6	2
1969	16	30	0	7
1970	43	19	1	1
1971	73	6	0	0
1972	34	18	0	0
Totals		**198**	**10**	**14**

"LeeRoy had determination and a no-quit attitude. He's right at the top of the list of the all-time great race drivers."

—*Junior Johnson*

WHY #32?

Yarbrough won 14 races in 198 Winston Cup starts. His best season was 1969, when he won seven races, all on superspeedways, and swept the Daytona 500, World 600 and Southern 500. Those wins pay a $1 million bonus today.

UGA

Born: September 17, 1938   **Raced out of: Jacksonville, Fla.**

The last owner/driver to win the Winston Cup championship, Kulwicki enjoyed his finest moment less than five months before his death in a plane crash on April 1, 1993. At the Hooters 500 in Atlanta on Nov. 15, 1992, Kulwicki finished second to Bill Elliott and earned enough points to edge Elliott for the series championship. Kulwicki's 10-point title margin was the smallest in Winston Cup history.

33

Alan KULWICKI

Born: December 14, 1954   **Raced out of: Greenfield, Wis.**   **Died on: April 1, 1993**

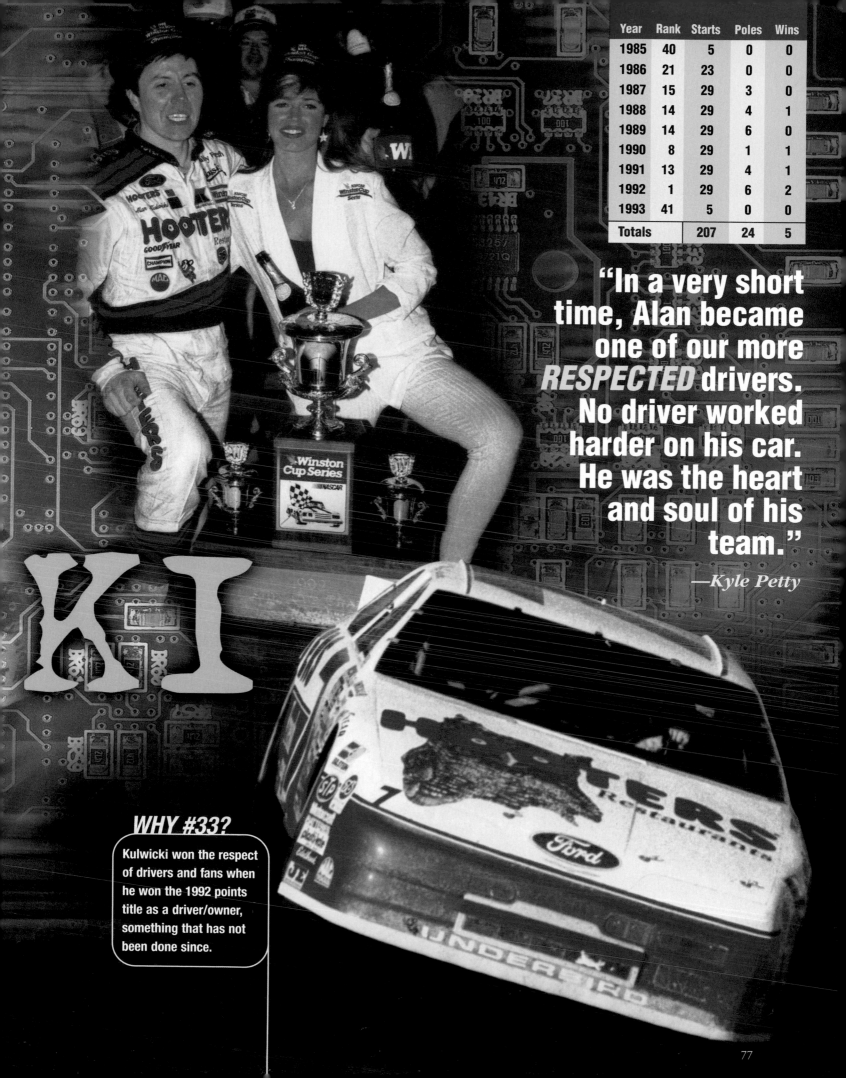

Year	Rank	Starts	Poles	Wins
1985	40	5	0	0
1986	21	23	0	0
1987	15	29	3	0
1988	14	29	4	1
1989	14	29	6	0
1990	8	29	1	1
1991	13	29	4	1
1992	1	29	6	2
1993	41	5	0	0
Totals		**207**	**24**	**5**

"In a very short time, Alan became one of our more *RESPECTED* drivers. No driver worked harder on his car. He was the heart and soul of his team."

—*Kyle Petty*

KI

WHY #33?

Kulwicki won the respect of drivers and fans when he won the 1992 points title as a driver/owner, something that has not been done since.

"Neil was a **great driver**. He was also as good a friend as anyone could ever find. Times with Neil were **always special**."

—*Dale Earnhardt*

Winner of 18 Winston Cup races, Bonnett began to realize his potential as a driver shortly after joining the legendary Wood Brothers team in 1979. After the eighth race of the season, Bonnett replaced David Pearson in the famed Mercury; four weeks later he collected his third career victory at Dover. Bonnett would go on to post victories at Daytona and Atlanta later that season.

Neil

34 BONN

WHY #34?

A member of the Alabama Gang, Bonnett won 18 races and was popular among fans and drivers. A crash in 1990 sent him to the TV booth, but he returned as a driver in 1993. During practice for the Daytona 500 in 1994, Bonnett was killed in a crash.

Year	Rank	Starts	Poles	Wins
1974	87	2	0	0
1975	NR	2	0	0
1976	32	14	1	0
1977	18	23	6	2
1978	12	30	3	0
1979	26	21	4	3
1980	19	22	0	2
1981	22	22	1	3
1982	17	25	0	1
1983	6	30	4	2
1984	8	30	0	0
1985	4	28	1	2
1986	13	28	0	1
1987	12	26	0	0
1988	16	27	0	2
1989	20	26	0	0
1990	43	5	0	0
1993	T67	2	0	0
Totals		**363**	**20**	**18**

ETT

Born: July 30, 1946   **Raced out of: Bessemer, Ala.**   **Died on: February, 11, 1994**

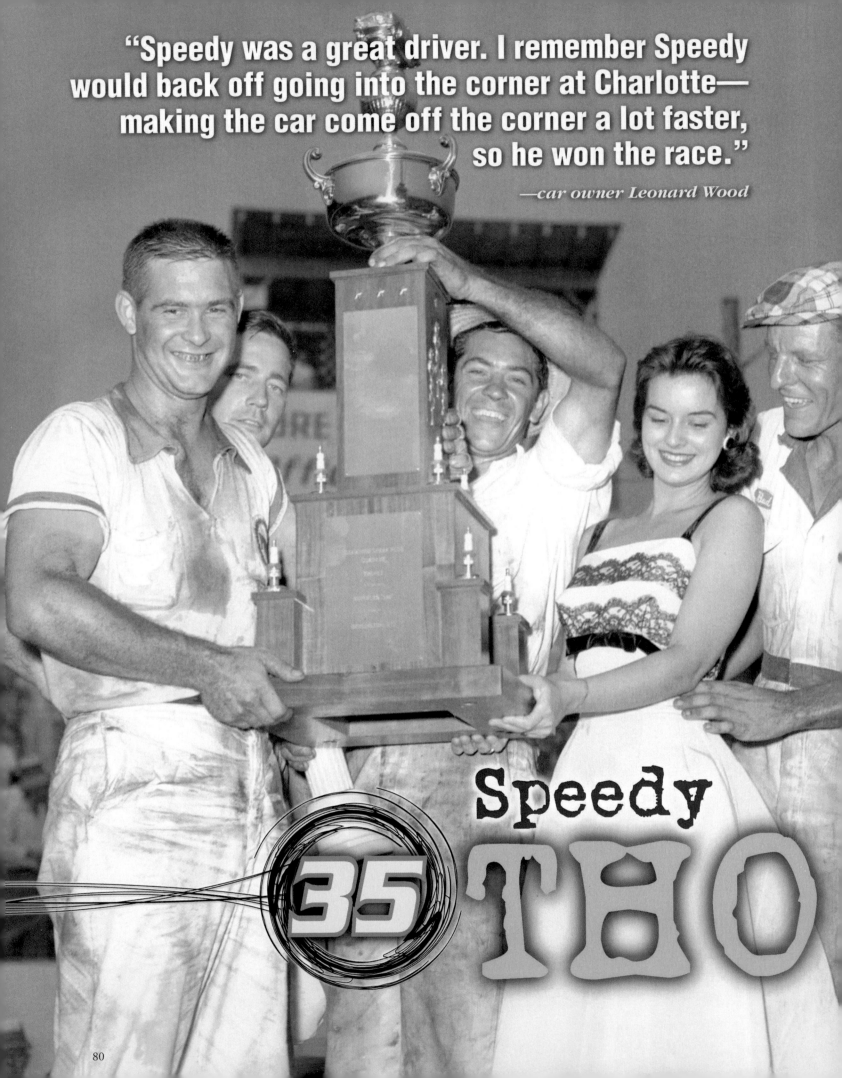

"Speedy was a great driver. I remember Speedy would back off going into the corner at Charlotte— making the car come off the corner a lot faster, so he won the race."

—car owner Leonard Wood

Speedy
35
THO

Year	Rank	Starts	Poles	Wins
1950	NR	1	0	0
1951	75	3	0	0
1952	37	2	0	0
1953	11	7	0	2
1954	23	7	0	0
1955	15	15	0	2
1956	2	42	6	8
1957	3	38	4	2
1958	3	38	7	4
1959	3	29	1	0
1960	25	9	0	2
1961	63	3	0	0
1962	41	3	0	0
1963	NR	1	0	0
Totals		198	18	20

WHY #35?

Alfred Thompson enjoyed his best season in 1958, when he accumulated eight of his 20 victories. He finished in the top three in points standings from 1956-59.

Driving for the Carl Kiekhafer/Chrysler juggernaut in 1956, the popular Thompson won eight races and finished third in the points race behind teammates Buck Baker and Herb Thomas. All told, Kiekhaefer-owned cars won 30 of 50 starts in 1956, including the last five races of the season. Thompson also finished third in the 1957 standings, third in 1958 and 1959.

MPSON

Born: January 16, 1935   Raced out of: Monroe, NC

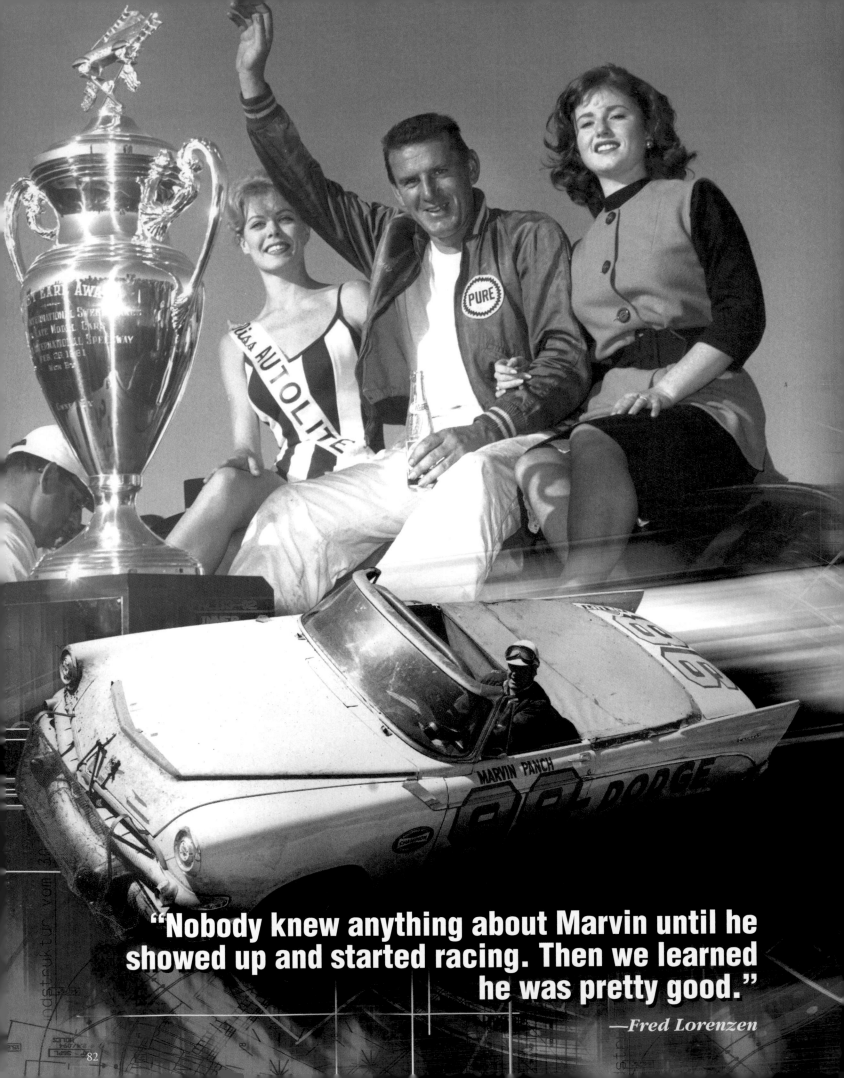

"Nobody knew anything about Marvin until he showed up and started racing. Then we learned he was pretty good."

—Fred Lorenzen

Year	Rank	Starts	Poles	Wins
1951	36	3	0	0
1953	60	2	0	0
1954	17	10	1	0
1955	14	10	0	0
1956	10	20	1	1
1957	2	42	4	6
1958	18	11	2	0
1959	66	4	0	0
1960	26	11	0	0
1961	18	9	1	1
1962	9	17	0	0
1963	13	12	2	1
1964	10	31	5	3
1965	5	20	5	4
1966	17	14	0	1
Totals		216	21	17

WHY #36?

Panch was the first West Coast driver to make a splash in NASCAR. As an unknown rookie in 1957, he won six races and had 27 top-10 finishes. Panch finished second to Buck Baker in the points standings that year.

36
Marvin
PANCH

Panch turned heads in 1957 with six victories and a second-place finish in the points standings. He loudly announced his status as a title contender by winning the first two races of the season, a 150-miler on the dirt road course at Lancaster, Cal., and a 100-miler on the half-mile dirt track at Concord, N.C. Later that same season, Panch added back-to-back victories at the Southern States Fairgrounds (Charlotte) and Memphis-Arkansas Speedway (LeHi, Ark.). In 1961 he added the coveted Daytona 500 title to his resume.

Born: May 28, 1926   Raced out of: Oakland, Calif.   Died on: February 11, 1994

Year	Rank	Starts	Poles	Wins
1963	NR	5	0	0
1964	NR	6	0	1
1965	NR	4	0	1
1966	NR	4	0	0
1967	NR	7	0	0
1968	NR	4	0	0
1969	NR	4	1	0
1970	NR	3	0	1
1971	NR	7	4	2
1972	NR	6	3	2
1973	NR	3	0	0
1974	44	4	0	0
1975	NR	7	0	0
1976	NR	5	1	0
1977	NR	6	1	0
1978	NR	2	0	0
1979	NR	2	0	0
1980	101	1	0	0
1981	59	3	0	0
1982	70	2	0	0
1983	76	3	0	0
1984	76	3	0	0
1985	45	7	0	0
1986	50	5	0	0
1987	49	6	0	0
1988	42	7	0	0
1989	40	7	0	0
1990	62	3	0	0
1992	70	1	0	0
1993	NR	0	0	0
1994	70T	1	0	0
Totals		**128**	**10**	**7**

"I've always respected A.J. for what he could do in any type of car—an open wheel car, a stock car or a sports car. He had a gift."

—*Richard Petty*

Born: January 16, 1935   **Raced out of: Houston, Texas**

Known primarily for his four victories in the Indianapolis 500, the no-nonsense Texan was a terror in a stock car. In 1972, the 37-year-old Foyt claimed NASCAR's grand prize when he finished more than one lap ahead of runner-up Charlie Glotzbach in the Daytona 500. Foyt's most significant win was his sixth overall in the Winston Cup series, and it gave the Wood Brothers their third victory in the Daytona 500.

37

A.J. FOYT

WHY #37?

Foyt drove in 128 Winston Cup races, never more than seven in a season, and finished with seven wins. Factor in his success in open wheel—he won four Indy 500s—and sports cars, and Foyt must be considered the most versatile driver of all-time.

TEXAS **DODGE** DEALERS

47

85

"You could put Tim Richmond in a covered wagon, and if it would steer to the left, he would get the most out of it. No doubt in my mind, Tim was the closest thing out there to Dale Earnhardt."

—crew chief Larry McReynolds

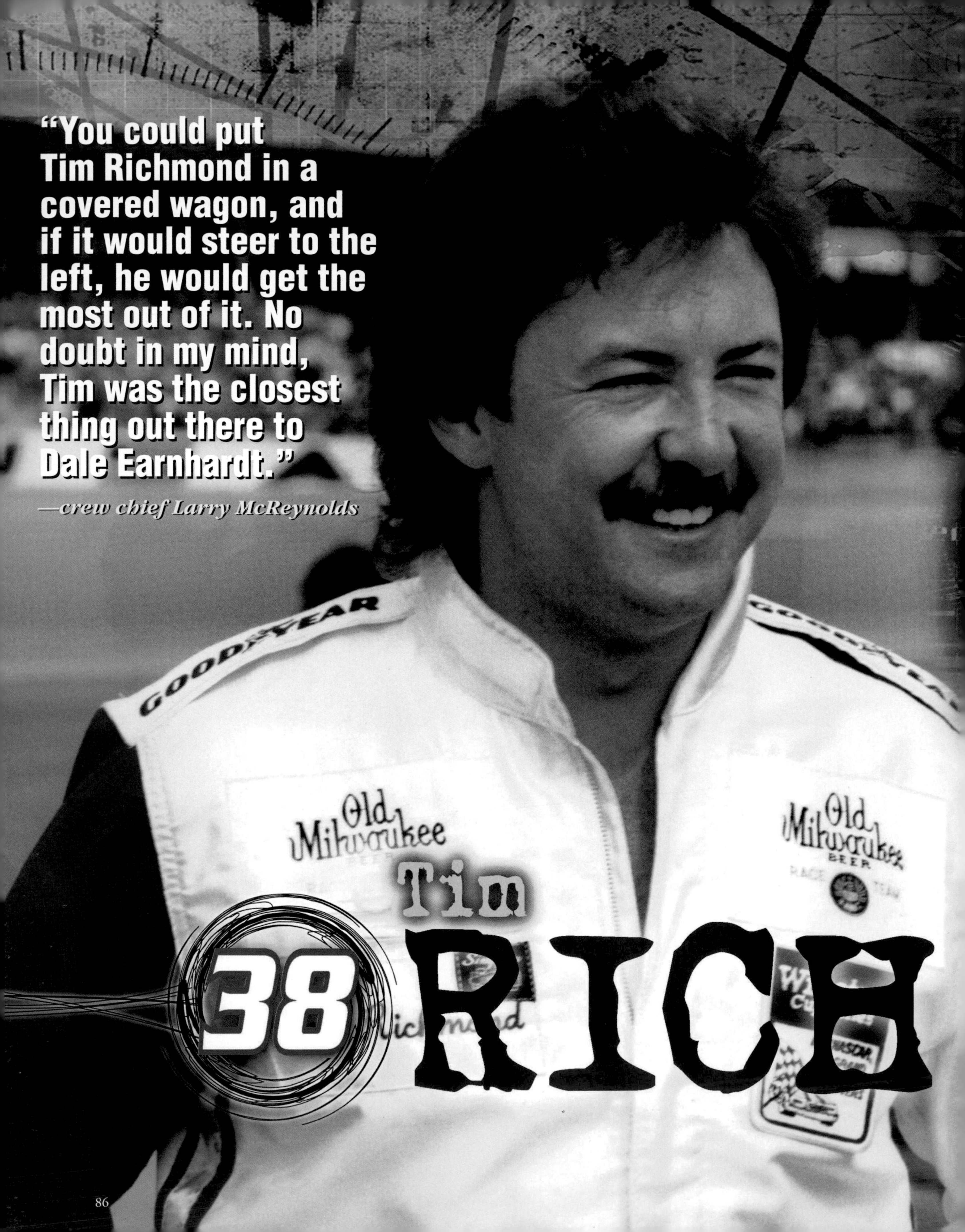

38 Tim RICH

One of NASCAR's most controversial stars, the unconventional Richmond could drive the wheels off a car. Though he enjoyed his most successful season in 1986—with a series-best seven victories and a third-place finish in the points—Richmond made a lasting mark on the sport with a triumphant return from an extended illness on June 14, 1987 at Pocono. Richmond won the race and triumphed a week later at Riverside, Cal. But the 1987 season would be his last as a driver. The illness that had been shrouded in secrecy—AIDS—took his life on Aug. 7, 1989.

WHY #38?

Most agree Richmond was the closest thing to Dale Earnhardt with his win-at-all-costs driving style. Richmond, especially good on road courses, won 13 races and was the top winner in 1986 with seven.

MOND

Year	Rank	Starts	Poles	Wins
1980	41	5	0	0
1981	16	29	0	0
1982	26	26	1	2
1983	10	30	4	1
1984	12	30	0	1
1985	11	28	0	0
1986	3	29	8	7
1987	36	8	1	2
Totals		**185**	**14**	**13**

Born: June 7, 1955   **Raced out of: Ashland, Ohio**   **Died on: August 7, 1989**

Tony

STEW

39

WHY #39?

Put out this list 10 years from now, and Stewart might be among the top 15—if he learns to harness his temper. He hasn't won a Cup title but showed his promise with a brilliant rookie season in 1999. He had 12 wins in his first three seasons.

"Tony is such an exceptional talent; he's like (Juan) Montoya, like (Ayrton) Senna; everything he drives he adapts to so well."

—*Johnny Rutherford*

Year	Rank	Starts	Poles	Wins
1999	4	34	2	3
2000	6	34	2	6
2001	2	36	0	3
Totals		104	4	12

ART

NASCAR's latest "bad boy" is enormously talented—so much so that straight-laced car owner Joe Gibbs is willing to overlook Stewart's petulant attitude and volatile temper. But no one can deny his accomplishments. In 1999, with a win at Richmond in September, followed by back-to-back victories at Phoenix and Homestead in November, Stewart became the first Winston Cup driver to visit Victory Lane three times in his rookie season.

Born: May 20, 1971 Races out of: Rushville, Ind.

"Ernie runs as hard as anyone in the game."
—Robert Yates

40

IRVAN

The high point of Irvan's star-crossed career was the 1991 Daytona 500, a crash-filled event that saw only five cars finish on the lead lap. Irvan's victory put Morgan-McClure Racing on the map, but as the season progressed, Irvan gained an unwelcome notoriety for his aggressive driving style and an unflattering nickname to match—"Swervin' Irvan."

Born: January 13, 1959   Raced out of: Salinas, Calif.

WHY #40?

Given a 10 percent chance of living after a practice crash at Michigan in 1994, Irvan returned to race again late in 1995. He was a hard charger who rubbed many the wrong way when he first joined the Cup circuit. He finished with 15 wins, three of them coming after his recovery from the crash.

Year	Rank	Starts	Poles	Wins
1987	52	5	0	0
1988	26	25	0	0
1989	22	29	0	0
1990	9	29	3	1
1991	5	29	1	2
1992	11	29	3	3
1993	6	29	4	3
1994	22	20	5	3
1995	48	3	0	0
1996	10	31	1	2
1997	14	32	2	1
1998	19	30	3	0
1999	40	21	0	0
Totals		312	22	15

The oldest of three racing Bodines from Chemung, N.Y., Geoff was the first of the carpetbagging brothers to make his mark on an essentially Southern sport. In 1986, Bodine won the crown jewel of Winston Cup racing with a convincing victory in the Daytona 500, after Dale Earnhardt ran out of fuel with three laps to go. Though absent from NASCAR's elite series in recent years, Bodine still has aspirations of adding to his 18 career victories.

Geoffrey
BODINE

41

WHY #41?

Bodine will likely finish his career with 18 Winston Cup wins. His best points finish was third in 1990. He gives himself credit for being the first 'Yankee, outsider, Northerner to break into NASCAR.'

"When I first saw him driving modifieds, I thought,
This is a guy who could go places."

—Jerry Cook

Year	Rank	Starts	Poles	Wins
1979	81	3	0	0
1981	45	5	0	0
1982	22	25	2	0
1983	17	28	1	0
1984	9	30	3	3
1985	5	28	3	0
1986	8	29	8	2
1987	13	29	2	0
1988	6	29	3	1
1989	9	29	3	1
1990	3	29	2	3
1991	14	27	2	1
1992	16	29	0	2
1993	16	30	1	1
1994	17	31	5	3
1995	16	31	0	0
1996	17	31	0	1
1997	22	29	2	0
1998	27	32	0	0
1999	27	34	0	0
2000	45	14	0	0
2001	68	2	0	0
Totals		554	37	18

Born: April 18, 1949   Races out of: Chemung, N.Y.

"He won the 1960 Daytona, one of the first races where the driver and crew chief talked to each other on a two-way radio"

—engine builder Bud Moore

Year	Rank	Starts	Poles	Wins
1949	58	1	0	0
1950	32	3	0	0
1951	39	7	0	0
1952	34	8	1	0
1954	64	6	0	0
1955	141	2	0	0
1956	21	15	0	1
1957	5	39	2	4
1958	5	39	4	2
1959	8	21	3	4
1960	14	13	4	3
1961	7	25	0	2
1962	4	51	7	5
1963	24	29	2	0
1964	81	4	1	0
Totals		263	24	21

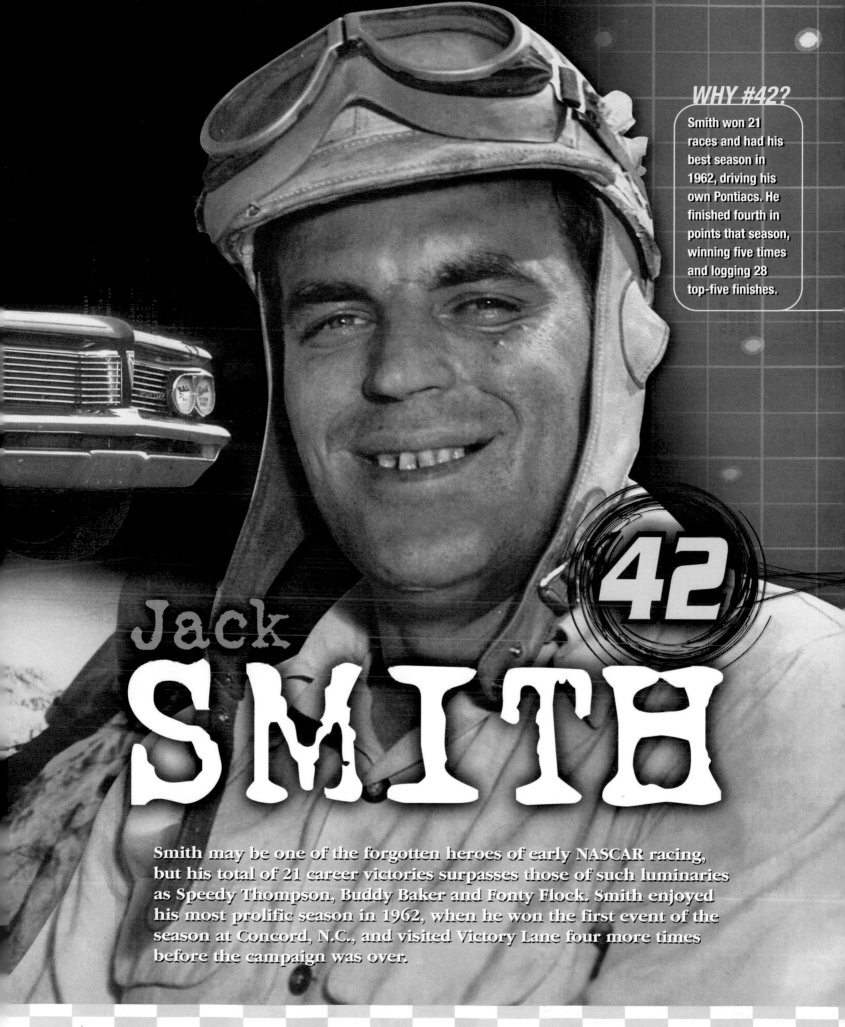

42

Jack SMITH

Smith may be one of the forgotten heroes of early NASCAR racing, but his total of 21 career victories surpasses those of such luminaries as Speedy Thompson, Buddy Baker and Fonty Flock. Smith enjoyed his most prolific season in 1962, when he won the first event of the season at Concord, N.C., and visited Victory Lane four more times before the campaign was over.

Born: May 24, 1924 **Raced out of: Sandy Springs, Ga.**

Year	Rank	Starts	Poles	Wins
1949	1	6	1	2
1950	NR	4	1	0
1951	NR	5	0	0
Totals		**15**	**2**	**2**

WHY #43?

The sport's first champion in the Strictly Stock Division in 1949, Robert Byron also won NASCAR's first sanctioned race. He finished with two wins and competed only one more season in NASCAR.

"Red was a very smart man and a very good driver who could have won a lot more races if he had stuck around longer."

—*Herb Thomas*

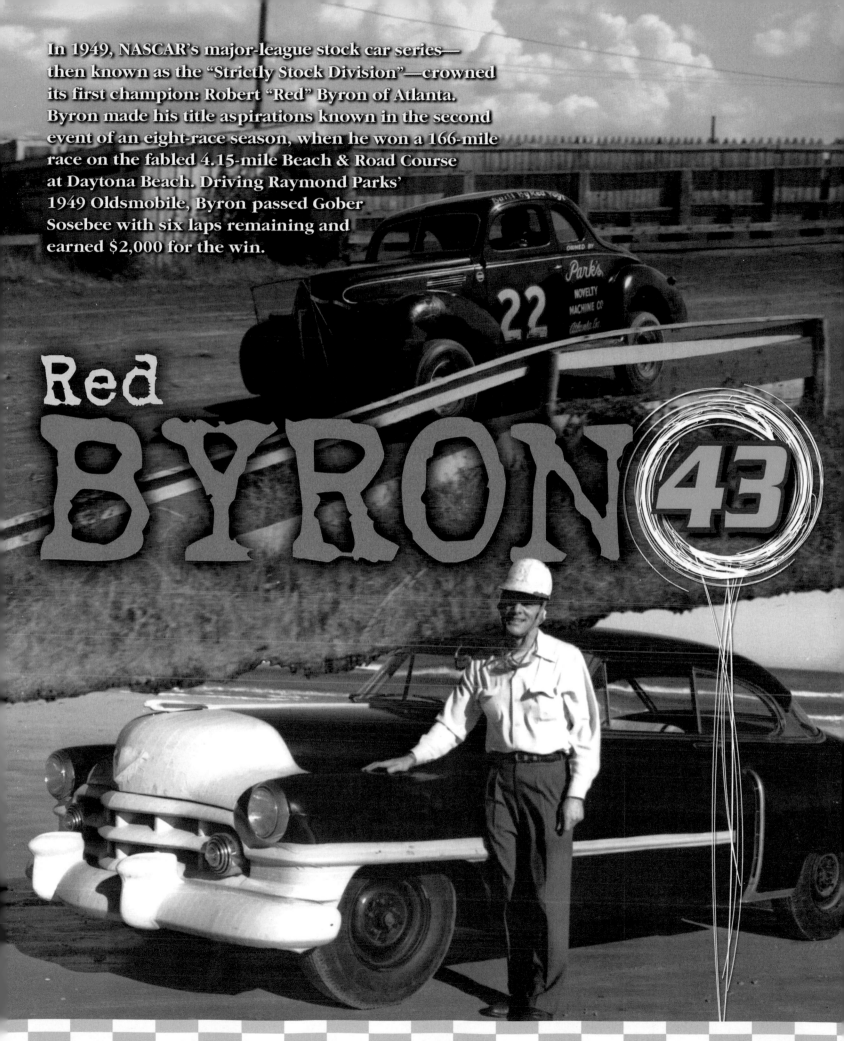

In 1949, NASCAR's major-league stock car series—
then known as the "Strictly Stock Division"—crowned
its first champion: Robert "Red" Byron of Atlanta.
Byron made his title aspirations known in the second
event of an eight-race season, when he won a 166-mile
race on the fabled 4.15-mile Beach & Road Course
at Daytona Beach. Driving Raymond Parks'
1949 Oldsmobile, Byron passed Gober
Sosebee with six laps remaining and
earned $2,000 for the win.

Red
BYRON 43

Born: March 12, 1915   **Raced out of: Anniston, Ala.**   **Died on: November 11, 1960**

Fonty FLOCK

The most flamboyant of the Flock brothers, Fonty was a pioneer among early NASCAR drivers. He collected a series-best eight of his 19 career victories in 1951, when he finished second in the points standings to champion Herb Thomas. After 19 races in an up-and-down season, Flock held the points lead before succumbing to Thomas' late-season charge. All three Flock brothers— Fonty, Tim and Bob —won at least one race in 1952.

"Fonty Flock had almost a Clark Gable look about him and could drive the wheels off a race car."

—*Buddy Baker*

Year	Rank	Starts	Poles	Wins
1949	5	6	0	0
1950	14	7	2	1
1951	2	34	12	8
1952	4	29	7	2
1953	5	33	3	4
1954	NR	5	0	0
1955	11	31	7	3
1956	50	7	2	1
1957	63	2	0	0
Totals		154	33	19

WHY #44?

Fonty wasn't as successful as brother Tim, but he won 19 races in 154 starts. Fonty, Tim and Bob, the oldest brother, all competed in the first NASCAR stock division race in 1949 at Charlotte.

Born: March 21, 1921   **Raced out of: Decatur, Ga.**   **Died on: July 15, 1972**

"The Marlins have no fear of bodily injury. I have been in the shop with them and seen Sterlin' pick up a cutting torch or a grinder and go right at it. I'm sitting there thinking he's risking a $10 million pair of eyes, but it never crosses his mind."

—*member of Marlin's pit crew David Edwards*

Year	Rank	Starts	Poles	Wins
1976	101	1	0	0
1978	67	2	0	0
1979	85	1	0	0
1980	49	5	0	0
1981	93	2	0	0
1982	NR	1	0	0
1983	19	30	0	0
1984	37	14	0	0
1985	37	8	0	0
1986	36	10	0	0
1987	11	29	0	0
1988	10	29	0	0
1989	12	29	0	0
1990	14	29	0	0
1991	7	29	2	0
1992	10	29	5	0
1993	15	30	0	0
1994	14	31	1	1
1995	3	31	1	3
1996	8	31	0	2
1997	25	32	0	0
1998	13	32	0	0
1999	16	34	1	0
2000	19	34	0	0
2001	3	36	1	2
Totals		539	11	8

WHY #45?

Coo Coo's boy is making a comeback. Marlin's career was on a downhill run until the 2001 season, when he finished in the top 3 in points. If Dodge continues to improve, Marlin might battle for the title in 2002.

Sterling MARLIN

45

In the first event of 1995, Marlin proved his 1994 Daytona 500 win was no fluke. Driving the Morgan-McClure Chevrolet at the peak of that organization's restrictor-plate prowess, Marlin outran Dale Earnhardt and Mark Martin for the victory. He would go on to finish third in the points standings in 1995. Sterling also equalled his best ranking of third in 2001.

Born: June 30, 1957   **Races out of: Columbia, Tenn.**

Donnie
ALLI

46

A member of the famed "Alabama Gang" from Hueytown, Allison drove throughout his career in the shadow of his more illustrious brother, Bobby. But Donnie had talent in his own right. In 1970, driving Banjo Matthews' 1969 Ford, he won his third race of the season, the Firecracker 400 at Daytona, after leader David Pearson blew a tire with seven laps remaining. In the 19 races he started that season, Allison posted 10 top-5 finishes.

Born: September 7, 1939   Raced out of: Hueytown, Ala.

Year	Rank	Starts	Poles	Wins
1966	64	2	0	0
1967	16	20	0	0
1968	25	13	1	1
1969	24	16	2	1
1970	40	19	1	3
1971	29	13	5	1
1972	36	10	0	0
1973	35	14	0	0
1974	17	21	2	0
1975	28	14	2	0
1976	34	9	0	1
1977	24	17	3	2
1978	25	17	0	1
1979	24	20	1	0
1980	26	18	1	0
1981	44	6	0	0
1982	41	9	0	0
1983	NR	2	0	0
1986	T114	1	0	0
1988	81	1	0	0
Totals		**242**	**18**	**10**

SON

Year	Rank	Starts	Poles	Wins
1950	13	3	0	0
1951	42	5	0	0
1952	65	4	0	0
1953	76	1	0	0
1954	84	4	0	0
1955	29	2	0	0
1956	52	8	0	0
1957	14	17	1	1
1958	17	29	2	1
1959	2	37	2	1
1960	39	14	3	1
1961	22	17	2	4
1962	30	16	1	0
1963	114T	1	0	0
1964	80	2	0	1
Totals		**160**	**11**	**9**

"Cotton was one of us in the sport who loved racing more than winning."

—*car owner Junie Donlavey*

WHY #47?

Cotton—because of the white hair—had nine wins and 18 second-place finishes in 160 career starts. Owens was crew chief of the Dodge David Pearson drove to his first Cup title in 1966.

COTTON OWENS

STEPHENS PONTIAC

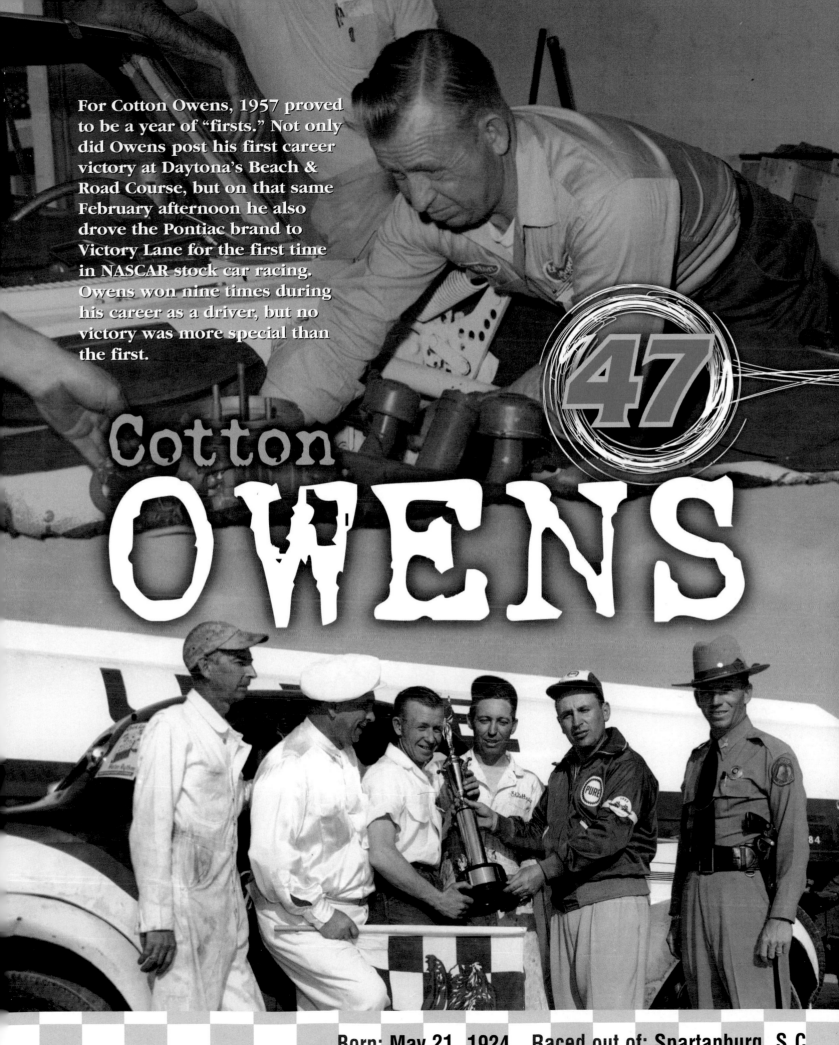

For Cotton Owens, 1957 proved to be a year of "firsts." Not only did Owens post his first career victory at Daytona's Beach & Road Course, but on that same February afternoon he also drove the Pontiac brand to Victory Lane for the first time in NASCAR stock car racing. Owens won nine times during his career as a driver, but no victory was more special than the first.

Cotton **OWENS**

47

Born: May 21, 1924   Raced out of: Spartanburg, S.C.

Tiny LUND

GOOD YEAR

48

Born: March 3, 1936   Raced out of: Cross, S.C.   Died on: August 17, 1975

"Tiny was a determined driver and the strongest, quickest, big guy you've ever seen."

—car owner Leonard Wood

Year	Rank	Starts	Poles	Wins
1955	217	1	0	0
1956	19	21	0	0
1957	11	32	3	0
1958	25	20	2	0
1959	20	25	0	0
1960	32	8	0	0
1961	23	10	0	0
1962	34	10	0	0
1963	10	22	0	1
1964	20	22	0	0
1965	21	30	0	1
1966	29	31	1	1
1967	19	19	0	0
1968	22	17	0	0
1969	NR	1	0	0
1970	NR	5	0	0
1971	NR	9	0	0
1972	104	4	0	0
1973	94	5	0	0
1975	116	1	0	0
Totals		**293**	**6**	**3**

It reads like a cheesy movie script. DeWayne "Tiny" Lund, one of the largest men ever to drive a stock car, rescues Marvin Panch from a flaming Maserati 10 days before the 1963 Daytona 500. Too badly injured to drive in the big event, Panch begs his car owners, Glen and Leonard Wood, to give the ride to Lund. The Wood Brothers stretch their fuel mileage, and Lund wins the Daytona 500 with one less pit stop than his competitors. Cheesy, perhaps—but it happened.

Teague, who won seven races, was known as King of the Beach for his success on Daytona's 4.7-mile beach road course. He won five times in 1951, his best season. He died in 1959 in a crash in a test session.

Year	Rank	Starts	Poles	Wins
1949	T62	1	0	0
1950	119	3	0	0
1951	NR	15	1	5
1952	NR	4	1	2
Totals		23	2	7

Marshall
TEAGUE

49

One of NASCAR's most colorful characters, Teague earned the nickname "King of the Beach" for his victories in 1951 and 1952 at the Daytona Beach & Road Course. Repeatedly at odds with NASCAR founder Bill France over his participation in races sanctioned by the American Automobile Association (the predecessor of the United States Auto Club), Teague was stripped of his NASCAR championship points—though he won seven of the 23 events he entered from 1949-52. Teague died in an Indy Car at Daytona in 1959, attempting to set a closed course speed record.

Born: Feb. 17, 1922   Raced out of: Daytona Beach, Fla.   Died: Feb. 11, 1959

"Marshall was really good on dirt. I liked his style so much that I kind of copied my driving style after his. He was real smooth."

—*Cotton Owens*

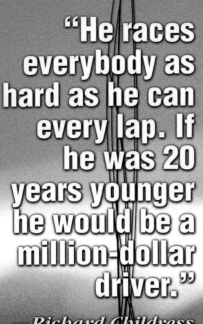

"He races everybody as hard as he can every lap. If he was 20 years younger he would be a million-dollar driver."

—*Richard Childress*

50

Dave MARCIS

A veteran of nearly 900 Winston Cup races, Marcis always chose to do it his way—from the shoestring budget he has to work with as an owner/driver to the wingtips he still prefers over state-of-the-art driving shoes. Though known for his independence, Marcis had his best season driving Nord Krauskopf's No. 71 K&K Insurance Dodge in 1976, when he notched three of his five career wins. A victory in the Talladega 500, where he finished 29.5 seconds ahead of Buddy Baker, was Marcis' first on a superspeedway. He followed that with a win at Atlanta in November.

Born: March 1, 1941   **Races out of: Wausau, Wis.**

Year	Rank	Starts	Poles	Wins
1968	34	10	0	0
1969	19	37	0	0
1970	9	47	0	0
1971	21	29	2	0
1972	15	27	0	0
1973	24	23	0	0
1974	6	30	0	0
1975	2	30	4	1
1976	6	30	7	3
1977	25	18	0	0
1978	5	30	0	0
1979	20	25	0	0
1980	9	31	0	0
1981	9	31	1	0
1982	6	30	0	1
1983	11	30	0	0
1984	13	30	0	0
1985	18	28	0	0
1986	17	29	0	0
1987	18	29	0	0
1988	19	29	0	0
1989	25	27	0	0
1990	21	29	0	0
1991	29	27	0	0
1992	29	29	0	0
1993	33	23	0	0
1994	36	23	0	0
1995	35	28	0	0
1996	38	27	0	0
1997	42	19	0	0
1998	45	13	0	0
1999	42	20	0	0
2000	46	11	0	0
2001	53	3	0	0
Totals		**881**	**14**	**5**

DALE
EARN

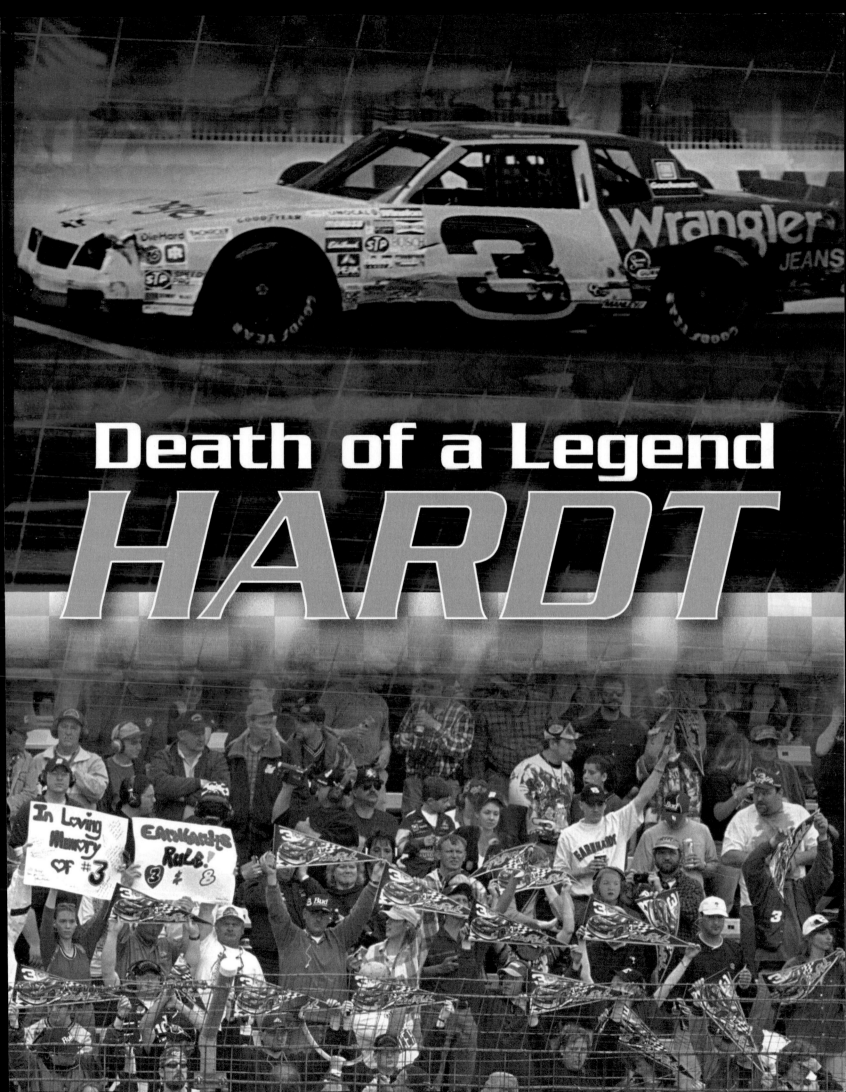

I walked past the driver's window of the No. 3 Chevrolet, and Dale Earnhardt waved, winked and flashed that unforgettable, mischievous, mustached smile.

Strapped tightly into his legendary black car and wearing the open-faced helmet he preferred for comfort's sake, Earnhardt was relaxed and affable that day—February 18, 2001—as he waited on the starting grid for his 23rd Daytona 500.

Never for a moment did I think it would be my last glimpse of his familiar face.

Earnhardt, the driver who won more races than any other at Daytona, the driver who amassed seven Winston Cup titles and 76 wins over a 25-year career—the driver who was husband to Teresa and father to Kerry, Kelly, Dale Jr. and Taylor Nicole—never made it to the finish line. He left the track in an ambulance, fatally injured. On the final lap, the man who understood the draft better than anyone else, backed off the lead pack behind Michael Waltrip and Dale Jr. to block the oncoming assault from Sterling Marlin, Ken Schrader and Rusty Wallace. Earnhardt knew that taking his opponents three-wide would open the door for Waltrip and Junior to battle for the victory.

This wasn't the Dale Earnhardt who many times said that on a race track his son was just another competitor. This wasn't the Dale Earnhardt who said he probably would bump Junior's No. 8 out of the way if the black No. 3 had a chance to win. This was the ultimate act of selflessness from

Dale Earnhardt was known as one of the best at drafting on the race tracks. Every driver needed to know where the Number 3 car was on the track.

Earnhardt had seven Winston Cup championships to his name, and was looking to win his eighth before his untimely death.

a driver who began the season with the belief he would win his eighth Winston Cup championship.

That act of selflessness might have cost him his life.

Marlin, with an excellent chance to break a 149-race winless streak if he could get past Earnhardt, was doing his best to make a move. Earnhardt was doing his best to hold him off. As the cars roared into Turn 4, they bumped, and the No. 3 careened out of control and hit the concrete retaining wall with a brutal impact.

On the radio, silence.

Richard Childress, Earnhardt's team owner since 1984 and his friend before that, got no response to his anxious radio call to his driver's headset. Childress sent teammate Mike Skinner to the scene of the wreck. Still nothing. He radioed to Teresa ... to crew chief Kevin Hamlin ... someone, anyone, to get an answer, but nothing came.

In victory lane, Michael Waltrip, the newest member of the team Earnhardt owns, was celebrating his first Winston Cup win in 463 starts. The emotion

Earnhardt considered his son just another competitor on the race track, but at the time of his death he was holding off the other drivers so that his son Dale Jr. and Michael Waltrip could race—just the two of them—to determine the winner.

between the brothers Waltrip—Darrell called the race from the television booth—was the highlight of the Fox broadcast.

No one knew that NASCAR's foremost driver sat lifeless as paramedics struggled to cut him from his wrecked car, which had come to rest on the grass in the tri-oval portion of the track. Earnhardt did not respond to efforts to revive him, and he was pronounced dead at 5:14 p.m. at nearby Halifax Medical Center.

Nicknamed "The Intimidator" because of his racing style, Earnhardt did everything possible to promote NASCAR. Earnhardt would never do anything to tarnish his family name or the good name of NASCAR.

"NASCAR has lost its greatest driver ever, and I have lost a dear friend," said NASCAR chairman Bill France Jr.

• • •

As a young man, Earnhardt's potential was obvious to France. Early in 2001, France talked from his heart about the contribution Earnhardt had made to the sport that the France family founded and even more about the respect he had for Earnhardt as a man.

And next to his father, Ralph, who died in 1973 before getting to see his son race in Winston Cup competition, it was France whom Earnhardt admired most.

"He helped me grow," Earnhardt had said the month before his fatal crash. "He helped me understand the sport better. Bill has always been a

Dr. Steve Bohannon, the director of emergency medical services at Daytona, made the announcement of Dale Earnhardt's death.

knew him best, said that part of the success was selling "Earnhardt" the image—The Intimidator, who was feared on and off the track. Yet if Earnhardt respected someone and gained that person's trust, one couldn't ask for a truer friend.

Earnhardt also was a NASCAR loyalist. Despite the safety issues, despite the uneven distribution of TV money and despite any inequities among the manufacturers, Earnhardt refused to tarnish the name of the family or the sport that made him.

In a January 2001 interview, Benny Parsons spoke of how much Earnhardt had evolved and matured since joining the Winston Cup ranks as a rookie in 1979.

"When he first came on the scene, I said he can't pull off representing a big company," Parsons said. "And boy, was I wrong there. Then I said he can't be consistent enough to win a championship—he's too much of a hard charger, he runs too hard to win championships. And once again, I was wrong. He has been really, truly amazing with how he has grown as far as his ability to speak and get up in front of people and be very candid. He's also been amazing on the race track.

"I think Earnhardt has more fans than any one driver. I wouldn't dare say he has more than all the other drivers combined, but if you interviewed every fan that came through the gates for the

great leader and a great philosopher. The interesting thing about Bill is that he doesn't forget anything about people. He remembers a person's name, who they are, what they do and what they said, for that matter ... in 1940. He's been there. He's seen it. He's been up against these situations, and he knows what to expect and how to handle it."

Although it was Earnhardt who laid the groundwork for a formidable motorsports dynasty, it was the guidance of "Billy" that took the scruffy factory worker from Kannapolis, N.C., and turned him into a legend. Earnhardt's wife, Teresa, who

Daytona, February 18, 2001 was Dale Earnhardt's last race as he slammed into the wall on the final turn.

Daytona 500 and they gave you an honest answer, I think Earnhardt would total up more than anyone else. Any time you have somebody that popular—like Richard Petty or David Pearson—then, yes, they have a dramatic impact on the sport."

• • •

Childress and Earnhardt were just two simple racers from North Carolina. Off the track, they were friends. The two hunted and fished and enjoyed life. Childress often said their relationship was based on "the tremendous respect" they had for each other.

"It doesn't matter what it is, he doesn't like to lose," Childress once said. "He just has a competitive nature. When you get down to the last 50 laps of a race, he knows how to dig deeper than any driver I know to make things happen."

Earnhardt had a work ethic second to none.

The flag is flown at half-staff just hours after Dale Earnhardt's fatal crash at the Daytona 500.

He didn't give handouts to his first three children, choosing to share that same lesson with them. Kerry and Junior had to work at Earnhardt's Chevrolet dealership and on their own cars before earning the right to race—just as Dad had. Earnhardt's oldest daughter, Kelly, raced as well,

but she is currently a successful businesswoman with Action Performance, a racing collectibles business. Whenever Earnhardt spoke of Kelly's newborn daughter, a softness that was unmatched came over his face.

Finally, with 12-year-old Taylor Nicole,

Benny Parsons said that Earnhardt "has more fans than any one driver." The fans showed their support for their fallen hero for weeks following his crash.

The next day when she got home from school, she and Dad took a spin around the farm in her new Corvette. Earnhardt pointed to the car and bragged about how Taylor already was becoming a great little driver, how she parked the car perfectly on the showroom floor. Then he said how proud he was of all his children and how far they had come. He described the struggles of building Dale Earnhardt Inc., but he said it was worth it to ensure his children's future.

Earnhardt had a chance to be the father he didn't have time to be to his other children. It wasn't unusual when Earnhardt was in town to see him pick up Taylor from school or take her deer hunting on the family's 300-acre farm in Mooresville, N.C.

When I talked to Earnhardt early in 2001, he could hardly contain his excitement of finding a vintage 1988 Corvette for Taylor—the year she was born. He spoke of the low miles on the car and how it took him a year to find just the right one. She had a dream that "Daddy" had bought her a car.

"In the grand scheme of things, it's unique to have all this, but I feel that Dale Earnhardt Jr. one day will be able to step in and run all this, and hopefully Kelly and Kerry and Taylor will all be involved too," Earnhardt said. "They'll all run this and race out of here and then do great. Hopefully after I retire from driving, I'll be a great car owner for several years, then I can turn this over to the kids and let them run it and race on."

Earnhardt memorabilia sales skyrocketed as fans clammored to get their hands on any piece of Earnhardt merchandise so they could remember their favorite driver.

• • •

Fans in the infield at the Daytona 500 were in disbelief on that sad day in February. "It's awful," said Kimberly Bennett, an Earnhardt fan who, with her dad, Neil, was wheeling away two souvenir tires from Earnhardt Jr.'s pit. "It makes your heart hurt, just thinking about it."

"It's put a shadow over this whole speedway," said Neil Bennett, 41. "It's a tremendous loss to motorsports."

Kimberly drives Legends series cars in her native Stockton, Ga., and recently had painted her No. 21 car to look exactly the same as Earnhardt's No. 3, down to the black, white and red paint job. "I liked the way he talked when he came out of the car," said Kimberly, 15. "He always had something nice to say. And he was real competitive."

Ned Jarrett, winner of 50 races over a 13-year career in Winston Cup racing, says Earnhardt was a champ. "In my opinion, and I've said this many

130

Fans from all over erected a shrine in Morresville, N.C., the place Earnhardt and his family called home.

for what he could do with a race car."

Jarrett has seen a lot of lives lost during his involvement with the sport. Earnhardt's death was the fourth in NASCAR series racing in 13 months. "It's just so hard to accept they're not there anymore," Jarrett said. "When you lose someone who accomplished so much to get the sport where it is today, it's tough. The man was dedicated to what he did. Every time he strapped himself into the race car, he went as hard as he could."

Jarrett said NASCAR didn't need to re-evaluate its safety policy. "NASCAR does a good job of doing what it can to make those race cars as safe as possible," he said. "I guess you can only do so much. Certainly we've seen race cars torn up worse than his (Earnhardt's) was and watched (the drivers) walk away. What safety measures could have prevented his death? I have no idea."

• • •

times, he was the best race-car driver that ever raced," Jarrett said. "He had a tremendous amount of God-given talent, and he worked hard to get the most out of it. Everybody respected the man

Dale Earnhardt had reached a stage in his life

There was an outpouring of emotion and sympathy from all the Dale Earnhardt fans of the world.

where he was content. He couldn't fight middle age, so he accepted it and approached it with a grace that comes from a confidence that few obtain.

"Life changes as you go through it," he said. "Sure you have to focus on different things at different times in your career. I'm 49 years old, and I'm pretty comfortable in my life. Things don't really rattle me when someone comes up and says you're getting audited by the tax collector or you're losing a key member of the team or your sponsor is unhappy.

"What I do rather than get rattled is to analyze the situation, try to correct it or straighten the program out and go forward. A lot of things rattled me earlier in life, but as you get older, you get more experience. You try to take things in stride and have a good time."

Moments before his death, Dale Earnhardt was having a good time. He was mixing it up at Daytona, doing what he did best, loving every second of it.

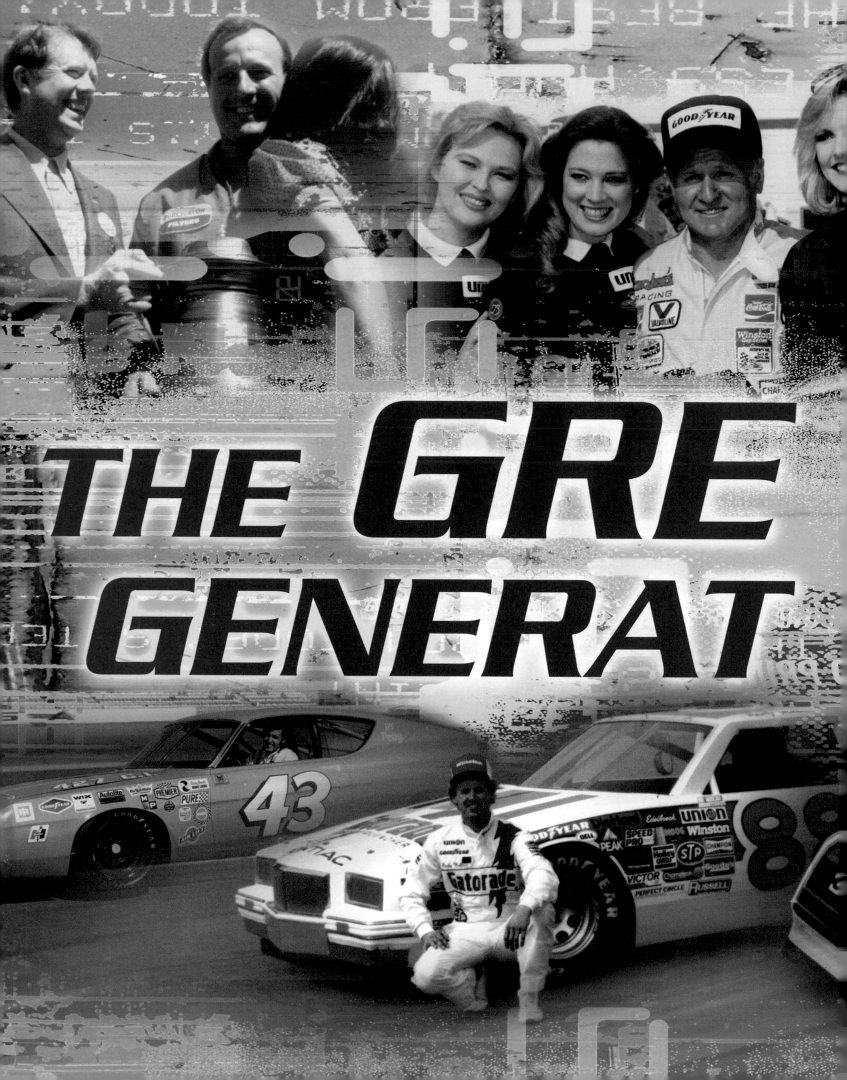

In 1978, President Jimmy Carter unofficially elevated NASCAR to the status of a major sport when he invited a group of drivers that included legends Richard Petty, David Pearson, Cale Yarborough and Bobby Allison to the White House. There was no way to know it at the time, but Carter was ushering in the beginning of NASCAR's Golden Decade as well.

For the next 10 years, Petty, Pearson, Yarborough and the racing Allisons would struggle to fend off the rise of the next generation of great drivers, a group headed by Darrell Waltrip and Dale Earnhardt, who were followed in short order by the likes of Bill Elliott, Rusty Wallace and Mark Martin. As old gave way to new, fans would be the ultimate beneficiaries, enjoying a non-stop series of bumper-to-bumper battles that would extend throughout the decade.

Along the way, a veritable "who's who" of great drivers rose to the top of the sport, most of whom landed at or near the top of the 50 Greatest Drivers list that NASCAR compiled at the end of the century. In the process, those drivers completed the task of putting stock car racing on the map as a mainstream sport, and they also built the foundation for the explosion in popularity to come in the early 1990s, when a young driver named Jeff Gordon completed the process by mounting a challenge to Dale Earnhardt's claim to NASCAR's racing throne.

Great statistics abound for the drivers from this illustrious decade, but perhaps the most noteworthy one is this: Of the 11 drivers who posted more than 50 victories over the course

President Jimmy Carter helped usher in the Golden Decade of NASCAR by inviting drivers to the White House such as Cale Yarborough (above).

Richard Petty was able to capture the audience's attention and lay the foundation for NASCAR drivers for years to come.

of their Winston Cup careers, eight ran between 1978 and 1988, and at least two—Waltrip and Earnhardt—were either in or approaching their prime. Those eight drivers compiled a total of more than 500 career victories, a number that swells by almost another hundred when the numbers of Elliott, Martin and Harry Gant are factored in.

Clearly, it was NASCAR's greatest era when it came to the presence of talented drivers who knew how to win. But their greatness was defined by more than talent and victories. Waltrip and

Earnhardt brought a new era of personality to the sport, and in the process they redefined the nature of the competition.

Fans had thrilled to the exploits of great drivers before, of course, and the late '50s and early '60s were full of daredevil legends. But many lacked the restraint and range of subtle skills necessary to run up top on a weekly basis, making it relatively easy for Richard Petty to emerge from the pack and dominate. Once Petty ascended to the top of the NASCAR pyramid, the '60s and '70s settled into the "Petty vs. Pearson"

David Pearson found himself battling Richard Petty on the racetrack Sunday after Sunday, trying to knock off Petty from atop the NASCAR racing world.

show, and as talented as some of their competitors were, they were hard-pressed to break the stranglehold that Petty held on the sport.

• • •

So who were these drivers who so captured the fancy of fans during NASCAR's pivotal period? Start with the talent and charisma foundation laid by Petty, who dominated the sport in the '60s and '70s with his cocky demeanor and trademark cowboy hat. Balance that with the modest, cagey Pearson, the so-called "Silver Fox," who was arguably the best racing strategist in the sport's history.

Petty and Pearson knew their duo act was a long-running affair, and fans were treated to Sunday after Sunday of day-long battles in which the two drivers traded paint and swapped leads.

The transition from a friendly show to a no-holds-barred competition was first signaled by the emergence of Yarborough, a fierce competitor who offset Petty's

Pearson, also known as the "Silver Fox," has been called the best racing strategist in NASCAR history.

domination by grabbing three consecutive Winston Cup titles (1976-1978) as the '70s came to a close.

Yarborough's fiery racing style foreshadowed that of the hot-shoes young drivers who were about to emerge to steal the thunder of Petty, Pearson and Yarborough. What these drivers brought to the table was some of the panache from the drivers of the early '60s that had been lost in the ongoing Pearson-vs.-Petty duels. Suddenly, the battle for the Winston Cup title evolved into a hotly contested affair rather than a two-man show with lap traffic.

The last year of the decade would mark the debut of the combustible Dale Earnhardt, who quickly perfected his bump-and-wreck passing style to take his first Cup title in 1980. As much of a personality as Earnhardt became, it was Darrell Waltrip who captured the spotlight for the next couple of years as his career peaked.

Waltrip had been waiting in the wings and laying a foundation for some time. While Petty and Yarborough were conducting their final championship runs in the late '70s, DW was learning to win races, averaging a half-dozen victories a year from 1977-1980. Arriving a few years ahead of Earnhardt, he entered the beginning of a power vacuum in which his youth,

stamina and strength gave him a distinct advantage over the fading giants. By the time the decade turned, he was able to parlay that advantage into back-to-back Winston Cup titles (1981, 1982).

As great a driver as Waltrip was, it was his style that was special. Unlike Petty, who used a modest, "aw shucks" demeanor to balance his cockiness, Waltrip played the media with the same acumen he used to pass his opponents, using the press to plant inflammatory quotes that he knew would get under the skin of his opponents. But the man who became known as "Jaws" for his outrageous mouth could walk the walk as well as talk the talk,

Cale Yarborough (left) grabbed three consecutive Winston Cup titles in the late '70s. Darrell Waltrip backed up all his talk with back-to-back titles in 1981 and 1982.

and his championship battles against Bobby Allison became the stuff of legend. Dirty tricks, hot racing and airing out racing grievances in the media became the order of the day as two of NASCAR's legends fought to the wire for the title.

The two years in which Allison and Waltrip fought for the title featured the growing influence of crew chiefs. The brash Waltrip was backed by cagey owner Junior Johnson, who knew every tech trick in the book when it came to getting an

Bobby Allison (above) dueled Darrell Waltrip week after week for wins and the championship in the early '80s. He won the Winston Cup title in 1983.

edge for his driver, and he wasn't above rolling an occasional tire out onto pit road to slow down Allison. But Johnson had a foil who was up to the task in Gary Nelson, the crew chief for Allison who went on to invent the roof flaps that saved lives in the early '90s before becoming competition director for the series.

Despite Waltrip's unique talent and chutzpah, his stay at the top of the ladder was relatively brief. Earnhardt was beginning to temper his early energy with veteran wisdom, and the fear factor he engendered was something that was unprecedented since the early '60s. Despite the beginning of his frustration at Daytona, he ran the Winston Cup table two straight years after Waltrip's final championship in 1985, setting the stage for his dominant run the early '90s.

What Earnhardt added was the nasty edge that Waltrip lacked. Earnhardt put fear into his competitors by pushing the unwritten rules—established in large part by the likes of Petty and Pearson—to the breaking point. With earlier champions like Petty, it was possible to admire them

Dale Earnhardt pushed the limits of the "unwritten rules" of NASCAR with his brash style when he burst onto the scene.

Although Petty was responsible for the early fan base of NASCAR, he raced well into the 1980s against the up and comers.

and root against them at the same time. But with Earnhardt, there was no middle ground, and he quickly divided the NASCAR fan base into those who loved him and those who hated him.

Earnhardt's driving style also did the same thing to his competition. Before he came into the sport, it was assumed that overaggressive young drivers would learn their lesson quickly once they were spun out by a veteran or two. But Earnhardt rarely backed down, and as his driving skills continued to increase it wasn't long before he

became the one driver everyone else on the track feared.

But Earnhardt brought a lot more to the table than just great driving skills. Capitalizing on his outrageous reputation, he took merchandising to a new level that became the model for not just NASCAR, but much of the rest of the sports world as well. His skills as a marketer and salesman were as formidable as his driving skills, and he laid the groundwork for NASCAR's business success with his talent as a merchandiser. Without

From Jimmy Carter to Ronald Reagan, Democrats to Republicans, NASCAR fans were coming from all walks of life. Dale Earnhardt helped lay the groundwork for NASCAR's business success with his own merchandise line.

Earnhardt's shrewd business approach off the track, NASCAR would never have achieved the level of popularity the sport has attained today, including a billion-dollar TV contract, major network exposure and coverage in national magazines, high-level websites and major daily newspapers (all of which had previouslytreated the sport as a regional entity).

• • •

The drivers of that decade produced a series of highlights that went far beyond winning races. The shift started in 1979, when the post-Daytona 500 fisticuffs between Cale Yarborough and the Allisons (brothers Bobby and Donnie) during CBS' first wire-to-wire live telecast of the event made it clear that something different was going on in stock car racing. That race has been widely recognized as the event that put NASCAR on the

Bill Elliott (above) won 11 races in 1985 and became NASCAR's first million dollar winner. He won 40 races in his career.

Elliott broke the 200 miles per hour barrier in 1987. With six wins, he finished second in the Winston Cup standings that year.

media map, marking the beginning of the sport's rise from regional force to national phenomenon.

And the hits kept on coming, both in terms of bumper-to-bumper action and notable achievements in which a series of drivers rewrote much of the NASCAR record book. Richard Petty marked the beginning of the Golden Decade in 1979 by winning his seventh Winston Cup championship, a record that will not be broken well into Jeff Gordon's thirtysomething years. When Dale Earnhardt was killed at Daytona in February 2001, he, too, had seven titles.

In 1984, the fading Petty finally emerged from his struggles to get NASCAR victory No. 200, setting

Harry Gant was a consistent driver in NASCAR, racing well into his 50s.

the mark at the Firecracker 400 in Daytona in front of President Ronald Reagan, a victory that cemented Carter's prescience in recognizing NASCAR's nascent popularity as a sport of the people.

But there was plenty of action between Petty's final Winston Cup championship in '79 and his last

At the age of 51, Gant won four straight races in September 1991.

trip to victory lane. Benny Parsons captured the public's imagination by posting the first official qualifying lap of more than 200 miles an hour in 1982, a mark Elliott surpassed five years later by turning a lap time of 212.809 at Talladega. Waltrip capped off his illustrious career in '85 with one of the sport's great comebacks, rallyingfrom a points deficit of 206 to defeat Elliott for the Winston crown.

Elliott captured the public's imagination in his own way, becoming the first million-dollar winner of the Winston No Bull series in 1985 while winning 11 races, and he went on to win the Winston Cup title in 1988. Also in '88, the Allisons had their last hurrah when Bobby won the Daytona 500 at age 50 and son Davey finished second—just months before a head injury in a

The GREATEST GENERATION

The 1979 Daytona 500, which ended in fisticuffs between Cale Yarborough and the Allisons (brothers Bobby and Donnie, above) put stock car racing on the media map.

wreck at Pocono cost Bobby all memory of the victory.

• • •

The greatness of the drivers of this era can in part be marked by those who were largely overlooked. Benny Parsons gained most of his notoriety as a media maven after his retirement, but he won 20 races over the course of his career, and he went into the decade as an established Daytona 500 champion who was still a threat to win races. Harry Gant became a star because of his run of four consecutive wins in September 1991 at age 51, but before that Gant was the logical heir to the racing technique of David Pearson, a cagey, remarkably consistent driver who was a threat to win every time he took to the track in either a Busch or a Cup car.

The young Mark Martin also earned his

152

Mark Martin's long and successful career that started in the 1980s has helped carry NASCAR into the present.

racing stripes during that era, and the flamboyant Rusty Wallace learned his stylish image-making from the best of the best as he came up during the mid-'80s. In any other era, these drivers would have become marquee stars in their own right, but in the 1980s they were simply overshadowed by

the incredible talent around them, and each would go on to have his day in the sun in subsequent campaigns.

With the images of Petty, Pearson and the Allisons fading in the rear-view mirror, the end of the era was marked by the death in 1989 of Tim

Tim Richmond was on his way to becoming one of NASCAR's top drivers in the late '80s when his career was cut short by the AIDS virus. Richmond was often called the closest thing to Dale Earnhardt with his win at all costs style of racing.

spot at the top of the heap, and it will make it even more difficult for the likes of Dale Earnhardt Jr., Tony Stewart and Kevin Harvick to unseat Gordon and establish a dominant run of their own.

Changes on the public relations side of the sport make it equally unlikely that a group of drivers with the personality and chutzpah of Waltrip, Earnhardt Sr. and Elliott will emerge.

These days, cookie-cutter comments from drivers are the order of the day, and drivers like Stewart and Harvick are vilified and fined for anything remotely resembling some combination of emotion, honesty and personality in what they say before and after races. Perhaps the pendulum will eventually swing back the other way, but for the near future the color, candor and talent of the generation of drivers who competed from the late-1970s
to the late-'80s will continue to mark that era as NASCAR's Golden Decade.

Richmond won 13 races in just eight seasons before he died in 1989.

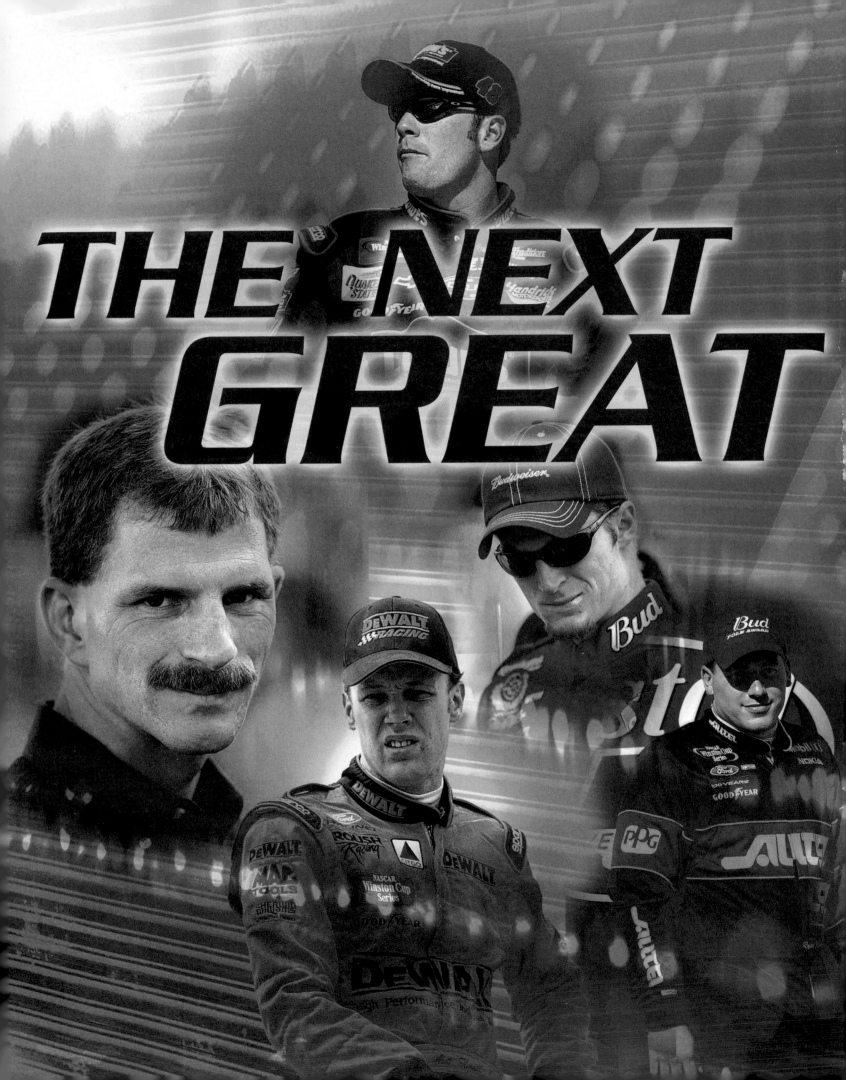

THE NEXT GREAT

ONES

The NEXT GREAT ONES

After Jeff Gordon won his first Winston Cup title in 1995, the search was on to discover "the next Jeff Gordon."

Not only were owners hoping to cash in on the next superstar, manufacturers and sponsors were demanding it from the teams. But it wasn't an easy task to find a charismatic, twentysomething phenom who was not only striking and politically correct, but also capable of winning seven races in a season and a championship to boot.

And Gordon continued to raise the bar. Two years later, at age 27, the "rainbow warrior" won his second title with 10 wins, eight poles, 22 top-five finishes and 23 top 10's. In 1998, in just his sixth season on the circuit, Gordon won his third Winston Cup championship and became the first driver since Richard Petty in 1975 to win 13 races in one year.

Gordon may be a "mature" 30 years old now, but he's still leading the brigade of NASCAR's youth movement. Many of the older drivers looking for Winston Cup rides say owners won't even talk to them if they have a three in front of their age.

Even Gordon, who recently announced the inception of his own Winston Cup team, chose 26-year-old Jimmie Johnson to pilot the No. 48 Lowe's Chevrolet full time in 2002. Johnson, a relative unknown from the Busch Series, collected his first career win in his 58th race when the tour stopped at Chicagoland Speedway in July, outshining the likes of Mike Skinner and Jeff Burton.

"Jimmie is 25 or 26 and maybe that's one of the reasons I

Jimmy Johnson, 26, is Jeff Gordon's choice as driver for Gordon's own Winston Cup team.

picked him," Gordon said. "He's not so young that he has to learn on a steep curve. He's young enough that he's got the youthfulness, but he's mature enough to handle things at this level.

"He's got that natural ability to drive the car. That's not something that I need to be coaching him on. He might have a question when we get to the race track about a line or a bump or whatever. That to me, really comes on its own. If I had somebody to prepare me for some of those things, I think it would have gotten me a few steps ahead at the beginning. As a rookie, that was the most nightmarish year I've ever had in a race car. And it was because I didn't know. I wasn't prepared. I'm thankful I got through it, but it was a pretty tough year for me."

Imagine what Gordon could have accomplished if he had been prepared. In the future, that will be the difference between those who succeed in stock car's major league and those who are left in the dust.

There are many young upstarts who will battle "Air" Gordon well into the millennium, but as hectic as the sport has become since the Winston Cup champ made his successful run for Rookie of the Year in 1993, not only will a driver require skill, but also the maturity to handle the demands of the job.

Ryan Newman, a Purdue alum, is a 2002 rookie candidate at the age of 23.

One driver with those qualifications is Penske South's Ryan Newman, a 2002 rookie candidate. Not only did Newman, 23, come through the USAC ranks like Gordon, he carries an engineering degree from Purdue. Newman is not boisterous or wild off the track; his performance speaks loud enough. He realizes that despite the sheepskin hanging on his wall, there is still a lot of schooling to be accomplished.

And Newman is the quintessential student, easy to take direction and quick to adapt to a situation. In

Kevin Harvick set a modern-era record by winning a race in only his third start.

the inaugural event at Kansas City.

If Newman has been criticized for anything on the track, it's his sometimes overly aggressive nature that has resulted in flak from Busch Series veterans. The crew of Mike McLaughlin was so upset after a skirmish with Newman at Darlington that it left the remains of the No. 18 chassis on the front lawn at Penske South in Mooresville, N.C., wrapped in yellow tape, signifying his rookie status.

But Newman's teammate, 1989 Winston Cup champ Rusty Wallace, believes that a rookie must come into the series and stake out his turf, while exercising the good sense of not throwing bravado in the face of a veteran driver.

"The young guys just have it naturally in them to be aggressive," Wallace said. "But it doesn't have to be your mission to go out there and do that all the time. It's just your mission that if someone does it to you, you have to go out and do it back to them to set them straight.

"I'd love to help Ryan all I possibly can. He's a really cool dude. He's all ears and he listens real

just his second Winston Cup start, Newman won the pole for the Coca-Cola 600, but he learned quickly about overdriving a car and wrecked after leading the first 10 laps of the event. Still, Newman has qualified for every event he has entered and, in five starts, managed to finish fifth at the boss' hometown track, Michigan Speedway, and second in his fifth career start in

well. He's highly educated, and I'm just really impressed with what I've seen in him so far. I haven't seen anything negative whatsoever. My gosh, all the runs he's had, you've got to admit that they've been pretty stellar with that world record he put in place at Charlotte Motor Speedway and with winning that ARCA race and doing as well as he's done everywhere else.

"He's definitely a talented driver, but he knows as well as everyone knows, we've both got to participate real hard and we've both got to give and take to make the thing work, and we've got to learn off each other."

For most of the season, the old-timers were extremely tolerant of Kevin Harvick, a remarkable talent from Bakersfield, Calif., who clawed his way through the Craftsman truck and Busch Series ranks before landing in Richard Childress Racing's alpha ride following the death of Dale Earnhardt.

Only 25, Harvick set a modern-era record by winning his first Winston Cup race in his third start and maintained his position among the top 10 in points despite missing the first race of the season and running for the Busch Series title. As his confidence increased, so did his boldness on the track. But he tangled with the wrong veteran when he spun out race leader Bobby Hamilton at Martinsville.

"RC's got a young kid with a lot of talent trying to fill Dale Earnhardt's shoes and thinks he is Dale Earnhardt, but he wouldn't make a scab on Dale Earnhardt's butt right now," Hamilton quipped after the event. "Earnhardt knows how to do it. He don't. Somebody will black them eyes for him before he does because Earnhardt had earned a lot of respect from everybody. It's just different now, it really is. The kid's got a ton of talent and he's going to do a lot for NASCAR. We're all mad right now, and we'll have to race against each other later on."

Still, Harvick can easily hold his own on the track, and upcoming battles between Newman and Harvick should be legendary. Despite their diverse backgrounds, there is a mutual admiration between the two and at times their driving styles mirror one another.

Dale Earnhardt Jr. won his first NASCAR race on his 12th try.

Matt Kenseth beat out Earnhardt Jr. for the rookie title in 2000.

push the envelope, see how far you can take things. Until you see how far you can push things, then you have to drive the wheels off.

"I think Ryan has really surprised a lot of people including me, but ... in my mind, Jeff Gordon's still the one you're going to have to beat week in and week out to win the championship in the next five or six years." Gordon is a given as an ongoing threat, but in addition to Newman and Harvick, you can't overlook Dale Earnhardt Jr. and the ever-controversial Tony Stewart. Other than Gordon, there is probably not a young driver with as much natural talent as Stewart, but his volatility has people questioning his staying power in a sport that is so dependent on public image.

"The future of NASCAR is with Gordon, Harvick and Dale Jr., but I don't expect Stewart to stay with Winston Cup," Wallace said. "He'll say screw that and go back to Indy Car racing because he just can't stand the politics."

There are those who think Stewart is bucking to get fired

"I respect Ryan Newman because this is racing and something that we all like to do," Harvick said. "Obviously, Ryan has raced hard in his division and I've raced the same way and I (can't) see that there is any reason to change that. But you still have to go out and see how far you can

so he can return to his first love, Indy Cars—especially with the demise of CART after the 2002 season. Still, during his short tenure in stock cars, the 30-year-old Columbus, Ind., native scored three wins in his first season—a rookie record—and finished fourth in points, far exceeding

Gordon's freshman statistics. In three years on the tour, Stewart has yet to finish outside the top 10 in points, but his future remains unclear. As one high-ranking NASCAR official said, "NASCAR is still bigger than Tony Stewart." Unfortunately, Stewart has not yet made that realization.

Earnhardt Jr. has had the benefit of growing up in the sport and experiencing firsthand the demands and responsibilities that accompany a Winston Cup champ. Junior himself won back-to-back Busch Series championships, but nothing can prepare you for stardom. As strong as Junior came out of the box in his freshman year—he won a race in his 12th start and appeared to be a lock for the rookie title—the pressure got to his team midway through the year and Matt Kenseth sneaked in and stole the rookie honor.

Junior regained his focus in the 2001 season and started the year off strong as the runner-up to teammate Michael Waltrip in the Daytona 500. Losing his father in the same event seemed to accelerate Junior's level of maturation and though understandably reclusive, he has gracefully settled into his role to carry on the Earnhardt name.

But who will be his competition in the future?

"I think people like Gordon, Harvick and Tony are already established at the top—you know,

Casey Atwood showed a glimpse of his potential with a tenth place finish at the Pennzoil 400. He also finished eighth in the 2000 NASCAR Busch Series.

guys that will run for wins and championships every year," Junior said. "I think Matt Kenseth is still great. He's just had bad equipment around him this year. Beyond those, you have a lot of young guys that have a lot of talent that just need to find the right fit with a team and gain some experience. I think Jimmie Johnson is going to be great, especially with good equipment there. He may be like Tony Stewart—not dominant in the Busch Series, but much more comfortable in a Winston Cup car.

Kerry Earnhardt should join his brother, Dale Jr., on the NASCAR circuit soon.

"Casey (Atwood) and Bobby Hamilton Jr. are two young guys that drive the hell out of the car. I mean, look through the Busch Series and there are a lot of good young drivers like that just looking for the right team to show their stuff. My brother Kerry and my buddy Hank (Parker) Jr. are great examples of guys that I think have talent, but have never been in a situation where they have the team or the sponsor that can help them show their true potential."

Having the right equipment and the right team behind any driver can make or break a career, but it is truly a bonus for youngsters to start out with the best. With top-notch cars and advisers, they usually can escape the pitfalls and bad habits that can develop on an underfunded team. What separates these successful youngsters from the pack is that each of them hails from organizations with winning records—assuring an accelerated learning curve.

Now the big challenge will be keeping the young guns content in the future. While the veterans have had to work long and hard to maintain their status and standard of living, younger drivers are enjoying instant affluence. But along with the fame, they have had to sacrifice much of the normalcy of their lives.

"I love this sport and everything around it," Harvick

said. "But it takes a lot of time, and there are a lot of things you have to do to keep pace with it along the 36 races and the sponsorship commitment. I don't know where I see myself going with my career, but I don't see it going that far. I've been doing this since I was 5 years old and traveling on national circuits. But I still enjoy what I'm doing and I'll keep doing it until I'm not having fun anymore. I don't know when that will be, but I honestly don't see it lasting to 45."

And even Jeff Gordon, who has been the poster boy for "how to succeed in NASCAR," has felt the grind in the past. While many drivers have maintained winning careers well into their 40s and 50s, Gordon doesn't expect his career to last that long.

"It's turning into a young man's sport where five or 10 years ago it wasn't," Gordon said. "Maybe the trends are going that way. I look at that in a couple of different ways. The car owners and sponsors seem to be looking for young talent, and that gives more opportunity to the younger guys. The speeds of the cars are increasing and the demand on your body is becoming more physical. With the amount of traveling we're doing, I just don't know how long you can keep that up. Some of the guys that start getting up there in age might start thinking that they don't want to do this in their 50s, or even in their late 40s.

Hank Parker Jr. is a future star of NASCAR.

"I'm 30. I don't know when those years are going to come for me when I start second-guessing and questioning. But as long as I'm healthy and competitive and I've got the desire— and I'm a part of a competitive team— I'm going to keep doing it. So I don't put a number or an age on it. When it comes, that's when I need to start thinking twice."

Richard Petty

Most victories

1.	Richard Petty	200
2.	David Pearson	105
3.	Bobby Allison	84
	Darrell Waltrip	84
5.	Cale Yarborough	83
6.	Dale Earnhardt	76
7.	Jeff Gordon	58
8.	Lee Petty	55
9.	Rusty Wallace	54
10.	Ned Jarrett	50
	Junior Johnson	50
12.	Herb Thomas	48
13.	Buck Baker	46
14.	Bill Elliott	41
15.	Tim Flock	40
16.	Bobby Isaac	37
17.	Mark Martin	32
	Fireball Roberts	32
19.	Dale Jarrett	28

20.	Fred Lorenzen	26
	Rex White	26
22.	Jim Paschal	25
23.	Joe Weatherly	24
24.	Ricky Rudd	22
25.	Terry Labonte	21
	Jack Smith	21
	Benny Parsons	21

Most poles won

1.	Richard Petty	126
2.	David Pearson	113
3.	Cale Yarborough	70
4.	Darrell Waltrip	59
5.	Bobby Allison	57
6.	Bill Elliott	51
	Bobby Isaac	51
8.	Junior Johnson	47
9.	Buck Baker	44
10.	Mark Martin	41
11.	Jeff Gordon	40
	Buddy Baker	40
13.	Herb Thomas	39
	Tim Flock	39
15.	Geoff Bodine	37
16.	Rusty Wallace	35
	Rex White	35
	Fireball Roberts	35
	Ned Jarrett	35
20.	Fonty Flock	34
21.	Fred Lorenzen	33
22.	Ricky Rudd	27
24.	Terry Labonte	26
25.	Jack Smith	24
	Alan Kulwicki	24

Most starts

1.	Richard Petty	1,177
2.	Dave Marcis	881
3.	Darrell Waltrip	809
4.	Ricky Rudd	731
5.	Bobby Allison	717
6.	Terry Labonte	709
7.	Buddy Baker	698
8.	Dale Earnhardt	675
9.	Bill Elliott	659
10.	J.D. McDuffie	653
11.	Buck Baker	631
12.	James Hylton	602
13.	Kyle Petty	585
14.	David Pearson	574
15.	Rusy Wallace	562
16.	Buddy Arrington	560
17.	Cale Yarborough	559
18.	Geoff Bodine	554
19.	Sterling Marlin	539
20.	Elmo Langley	533

Most championships

1.	Dale Earnhardt	7
	Richard Petty	7
3.	Jeff Gordon	4
4.	Darrell Waltrip	3
	Cale Yarborough	3
	David Pearson	3
	Lee Petty	3
8.	Terry Labonte	2
	Ned Jarrett	2
	Joe Weatherly	2
	Buck Baker	2

	Tim Flock	2
	Herb Thomas	2
14.	Red Byron	1
	Bill Rexford	1
	Rex White	1
	Bobby Isaac	1
	Benny Parsons	1
	Bobby Allison	1
	Bill Elliott	1
	Rusty Wallace	1
	Alan Kulwicki	1
	Dale Jarett	1
	Bobby Labonte	1

Mark Martin

INDEX

Alphabetical Roster and Index

ACKNOWLEDGEMENTS

Like a skilled pit crew, the success of this book depended on the talents of a number of people:

• Lee Spencer and Bob McCullough lent their expertise, their writing and reporting skills to bring you the stories about the drivers.

• TSN Senior Editors Jim Gilstrap lent invaluable assistance with editing and checking the information in this book.

• Pete Newcomb served as photo editor on the book, using images from TSN photographers Bob Leverone, Robert Seale and Dilip Vishwanat.

• TSN Assistant Editors David Walton and Jeff Paur compiled much of the information on each driver.

• Michael Behrens created the design of the book with input from Bob Parajon, which Matt Kindt and Christen Sager then implemented. Steve Romer led the prepress staff of Chris Barnes-Amaro and Dave Brickey, ensuring every image on every page looked as good as it could.

Special thanks should also go out to Dale Bye and Jim Gilstrap, who with the input of a number of expert editors and writers, compiled the list of drivers and provided the rankings. You can read their justification for their rankings on the individual driver pages.

Bibliography credit also must go to a couple of outside sources:

The Stock Car Racing Encyclopedia, edited by Peter Golenbock and Greg Fielden, and published by Macmillan, was used as reference for the drivers' statistical data.

The NASCAR Winston Cup Series 2001 Media Guide also was a source for statistical data. In some instances where conflicts existed betweenthe two, information from the Media Guide was used as the source.

Quotes used in the driver profiles are attributed to NASCAR 50 Greatest Drivers, by Bill Center and Bob Moore, and published by HarperCollins.

PHOTOGRAPHY CREDITS

The Sporting News Archives: 12T, 15B, 28, 33T, 51, 53, 63T, 72, 90, 91B.

Bob Leverone: 14T, 19B, 22T, 22R, 22B, 37T, 37B, 40, 41T, 41B, 47T, 52B, 54T, 54B, 55, 62, 63B, 70B, 71, 100B, 101, 110, 115, 117, 120, 125, 126, 128, 129, 130, 132, 133, 134, 160, 161, 162, 163, 164, 165, 166, 167.

Robert Seale: 3, 4, 15T, 19T, 46, 47B.

Dilip Vishwanat: 18, 36, 52T, 70T, 114, 116, 118, 119, 122, 124, 135, 169.

International Speedway Corporation Archives: 12B, 13, 14B, 16T, 16B, 17, 20, 21T, 21B, 23, 24, 25T, 25B, 26, 27T, 27B, 29T, 29B, 30, 31T, 31B, 32, 33B,

34T, 34B, 35, 38, 39, 42T, 42B, 43, 44, 45T, 45B, 48T, 48B, 49, 50T, 50B, 56, 57T, 57B, 58, 59T, 59B, 60, 61TR, 61TL, 61B, 64T, 64B, 65, 66, 67T, 67B, 68, 69T, 69B, 73, 74, 75T, 75B, 76T, 76B, 77T, 77B, 78, 79, 80, 81, 82T, 82B, 83, 84, 85T, 85B, 86, 87T, 87B, 91T, 92, 93T, 93B, 94T, 94B, 95, 96, 97T, 97B, 98T, 98B, 99, 100T, 102, 103T, 103B, 104, 105T, 105B, 106, 107T, 107B, 108, 109T, 109B, 111T, 111B, 138, 139, 140, 141, 142T, 142B, 143, 144, 145T, 145B, 146, 147, 148, 149, 150, 151, 152, 153, 154, 155, 156, 157, 168, 170, 171.

AP/Wide World Photos: 123.

Front cover: (left to right) Jeff Gordon (Robert Seale/The Sporting News); Richard Petty (Bob Leverone/The Sporting News); Dale Earnhardt (Bob Leverone/The Sporting News).

Back Cover: Dale Earnhardt (International Speedway Corporation Archives).

173

Other books in The Sporting News Selects Series:

Baseball's 100 Greatest Players

Football's 100 Greatest Players

Baseball's 25 Greatest Moments

50 Greatest Sluggers

BOSTON

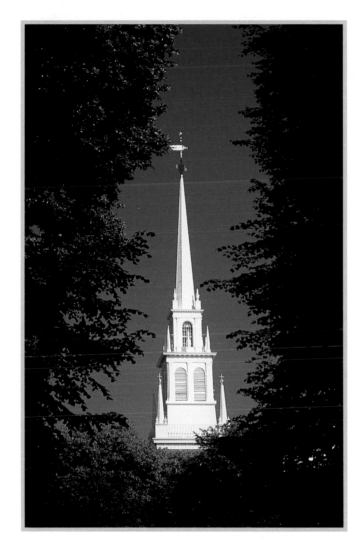

A PHOTOGRAPHIC PORTRAIT

Kevin and Susan Psaros

First published in the United States
of America by:

Twin Lights Publishers, Inc.
10 Hale Street
Rockport, Massachusetts 01966
Telephone: (978) 546-7398
http://www.twinlightspub.com

ISBN 1-885435-44-4

10 9 8 7 6 5 4 3 2

Cover: Image of Marriott's Custom
House used with permission of Marriott
International Inc, Marriott Vacation
Club International.

Text by:
Stan Patey

Book design by
SYP Design & Production, Inc.
http://www.sypdesign.com

Printed in China

INTRODUCTION

Explore Boston to appreciate the impact this remarkable city has had on an entire nation and the world. Boston birthed the American Revolution. In her noisy taverns and down her narrow and twisting streets the likes of Paul Revere, Sam Adams, John Hancock, and Dr. Joseph Warren quietly gathered to lead the colonies in revolution. Nowhere but Boston affords a view of so much American history.

The seaport that the Puritans founded in the late 1600's has all but disappeared beneath the surface of an ever-changing city. Expansion was imperative for the thriving city of the mid 1800's. So began the toilsome task of cutting down Boston's hills to fill in its waterfront. The city's area has more than tripled since then, but the layout of many of its streets, working their way around the period buildings, leaves the historical Boston easily discernable.

Boston is at once old and new. It is a city on the move, constantly remaking itself. Gaze down its seventeenth century streets and up at its mirrored skyscrapers. Stroll her public gardens and commons, explore the waterfront, thrill to Red Sox baseball and be inspired by runners in the Boston Marathon. Stand on the solid oak decks of the U.S.S. Constitution as sleek sailboats tack their way across the harbor steering clear of immense container ships. Everywhere you turn the old is reflected in the new.

Boston: A Photographic Portrait shares much of the city's history and beauty as seen through the eyes of Susan and Kevin Psaros. This book is an invitation to you to discover this delightful city, learn from it, enjoy it and take a piece home with you.

The Paul Revere House

The home of Paul Revere was constructed in 1680 and owned by the Revere family from 1770 to 1800. It is among Boston's oldest surviving buildings and now serves as a museum at 19 North Square in Boston's North End.

Quincy Market and Custom House

The Custom House Tower was added to the original custom house in 1913. The tower, with its sixteen floors was Boston's first skyscraper. The Marriott Corporation now uses the property for time-share condominiums.

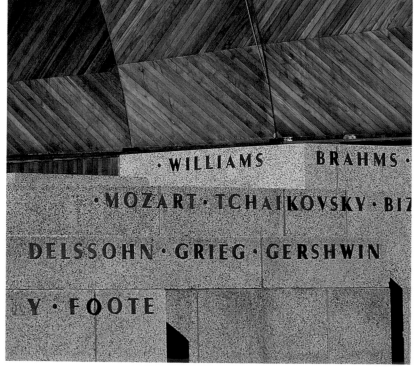

ABOVE

Arthur Fiedler Statue

Boston's beloved Arthur Fiedler conducted the Boston Pops Orchestra for fifty years. His statue is located on the Esplanade near the Hatch Shell where he entertained and delighted so many.

LEFT

Hatch Shell Detail

The names of famous composers are engraved in the polished granite risers that frame the stage at the Esplanade's Hatch Memorial Shell. The Shell is the summer home of the Boston Pops, Boston Ballet and a number of other performing groups.

OPPOSITE

Footbridge along the Esplanade

A runner takes a break to enjoy the beauty of America's first public playground. The seventeen-mile-long Esplanade follows the banks of the Charles River and is a popular destination for runners, walkers, rollerbladers and people looking to briefly escape the bustle of the city.

Autumn on the Esplanade

Autumn leaves color this tranquil Esplanade view.

Bull & Finch Pub

The Bull & Finch Pub at 84 Beacon Street was established in 1968 and is purported to be the inspiration for the television show *Cheers.*

Waterfront

The old and new of Boston's waterfront are framed in this shot. A well-preserved schooner and the Custom House Tower are contrasted by the modern skyline and the dinner cruise ship Odyssey.

Public Gardens

The Public Gardens were reclaimed from marshland
in the mid 1800's and now provide a quiet sanctu-
ary within the city and are home to the Swan Boats.

Copley Plaza Hotel

The Fairmont Copley Plaza Boston is reflected in
its neighbor the John Hancock Tower. Both are situated adjacent to Copley Square. This luxury hotel
has been in operation since 1912.

ABOVE

Trinity Church Detail

Expressive carvings adorn the sandstone and granite construction of Trinity Church. Since the ground beneath is too soft to support buildings, the Trinity Church is supported on some 4,000 cedar pilings driven down through the soft soil to bedrock below the former bay.

LEFT

South End

Boston's South End is home to 35,000 residents and boasts the largest collection of bow-front Victorian row houses anywhere in the United States. Like the Back Bay, the majority of the South End is filled land with its buildings constructed on wooden pilings.

OPPOSITE

Copley Square

Copley Square is named for John Singleton Copley, a renowned Boston Painter. The Trinity Church on the left was constructed in 1872 after the fifty-year long project to fill Back Bay was completed. The sixty-story John Hancock Tower looming in the background was constructed in 1976.

Frog Pond

Children frolic in the Frog Pond Wading Pool on
Boston Common.

Copley Square

Copley Square was reconstructed in 1969. Features
of the design include planted banks that shield the
park from its busy surrounds but do not block
views of its historic neighbors.

Community Boating, Inc.

Community Boating on the Charles River was established in 1936 by Joseph Lee, Jr. as a public sailing program and summer diversion for children. Pictured above is their fleet of dry-sailed 420 sailboats. The program now serves thousands of members.

Museum of Science

A World War II era amphibious landing craft adopted by Boston Duck Tours cruises past the Museum of Science on the Charles River. More than 1.6 million people visit the museum annually. The museum boasts an Imax theatre and planetarium as well as some 400 interactive exhibits.

Cathedral of the Holy Cross

Archbishop John J. Williams dedicated the Cathedral of the Holy Cross in 1875. Located at 1400 Washington Street, it accommodates 2000 parishioners and features a collection of beautiful stained glass windows.

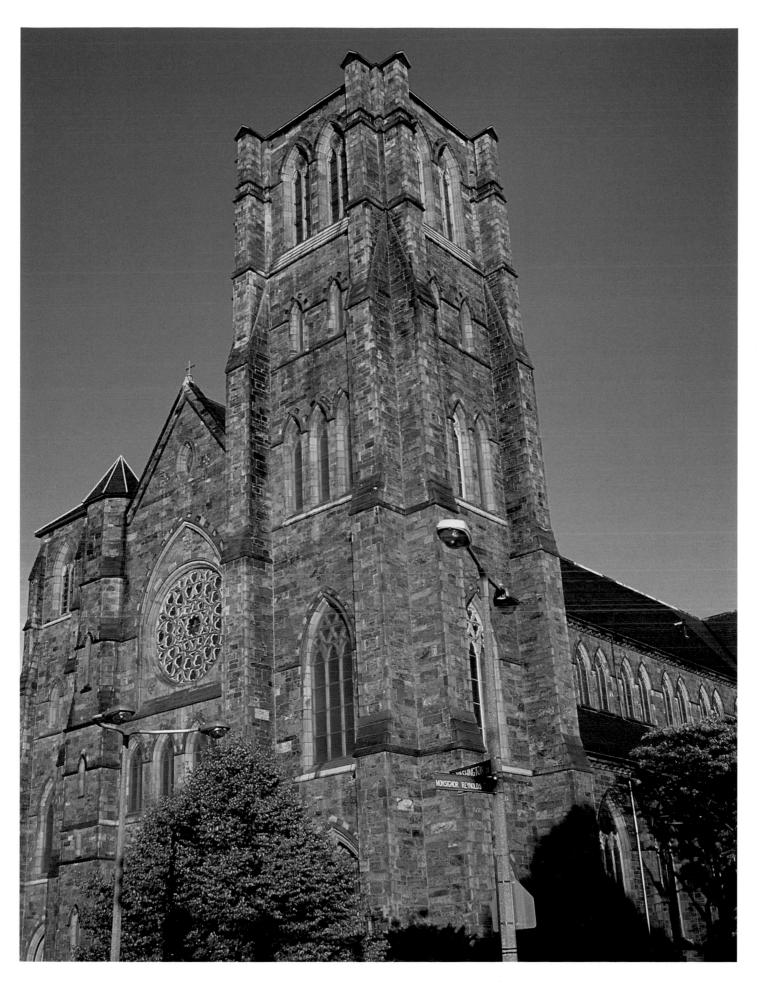

General Hooker

Major General Joseph Hooker served as the third commander of the Army of the Potomac during the civil war. This statue is located adjacent to the East Wing of the State House on Beacon Street.

LEFT

Storrow Drive, Back Bay

The Back Bay is reflected in the Charles River along Storrow Drive.

OPPOSITE

Bunker Hill Monument

The Bunker Hill Monument stands 221 feet tall and commemorates the June 17, 1775 battle. The first monument on the site was an 18-foot wooden pillar erected in 1794 by King Solomon's Lodge of Masons to honor fallen patriot and mason, Dr. Joseph Warren.

LEFT

King's Chapel Burying Ground

The King's Chapel Burying Ground is the oldest graveyard in Boston. It is the resting place of many of Boston's early residents including William Dawes who rode ahead of Paul Revere in April 1775 as well as governor John Winthrop.

RIGHT

King's Chapel

King James II ordered that the church be built in Boston to assure a presence of the Church of England. As no colonists were interested in selling land for the project a corner of the burial ground was taken and the church was constructed in 1686.

OPPOSITE

George Washington Statue

Created by Thomas Ball in 1869, this statue of George Washington astride his horse Nelson is located at the Arlington Street entrance to the Public Gardens.

The Lexington

The replica riverboat Lexington cruises the Charles
River with sightseeing and dinner tours. The trademark towers of the Longfellow Bridge stand in the
background.

The Esplanade

A view of the Charles River and Cambridge shores from beneath a weeping willow tree on the Esplanade.

Strolling the Espanade

Walkers along the Esplanade frame two small
sailboats tacking up the Charles River.

Boston Skyline from Cambridge

This view of Boston from the Cambridge shores captures the original 1947 art deco John Hancock Tower on the left and the new 1976 glass walled John Hancock Tower on the right.

Newbury Street Artists

Colorful prints are displayed on a Newbury Street corner.

Restaurant and Gallery

Newbury Street is populated with dozens of fine galleries and restaurants.

First Baptist Church

Henry Hobson Richardson designed the First Baptist Church at 110 Commonwealth Avenue in the Back Bay. Sculpted figures at the top of the tower depict baptism, communion, marriage and death.

North End Market

Boston's North End is famous for its Italian restaurants and shops. Mom & pop markets like this one are common.

Harvard Square Flower Shop

Harvard Square in Cambridge is home to a variety of interesting shops and restaurants. The open doors of this flower shop beckons visitors inside.

ABOVE

Swan Boats

In 1877 Robert Paget created the swan boats, which are still operated by his descendents. The swan was originally designed to cover the pedaling captains aboard these foot propelled boats.

OPPOSITE

Public Gardens

The Boston Public Gardens, established in 1837, is the oldest public park in the United States. Here a flowery oasis thrives in the heart of the city.

ABOVE

Boston Public Library

Established in 1848, the Boston Public Library was the first publicly funded municipal library in the United States. The pictured McKim Building is a National Historic Landmark on Copley Square.

LEFT

Boston Public Library Mural

John Singer Sargent created the Triumph of Religion mural cycle between 1890–1919. This is one of the many murals on display at the library.

OPPOSITE

Newbury Street Apartments

Newbury Street runs from the Public Gardens to Charlesgate. These eight blocks are distinguished by a variety of architectural styles.

The State House

The 1787 Bulfinch design for the State House
created a landmark for visitors and residents alike.
Governor Samuel Adams and Paul Revere laid the
cornerstone for the statehouse in a Masonic cere-
mony on July 4, 1795.

Golden Dome

Architect Charles Bulfinch intended the dome of
Boston's State House to distinguish the building.
Unfortunately the wooden roof leaked and had to
be sheathed in copper by coppersmith Paul Revere.
The dome has been painted a variety of colors but
was most recently re-gilded in gold in 1997.

The Museum of Fine Arts

Cyrus Edwin Dallin's *Appeal to the Great Spirit*
marks the entrance of Boston's Museum of Fine
Arts on Huntington Avenue.

Massachusetts Horticultural Hall

The Massachusetts Horticultural Hall has served as
an exhibition hall, contained a library and following
its recent renovation now serves as the offices for
Boston Magazine.

Turtle

As a tribute to runners in the Boston Marathon who run to finish Nancy Schon created the Tortoise and Hare sculptures at Copley Square. The finish line for the 26.2 mile race crosses Boylston Street just a few yards away.

Old North Church

Two lanterns were placed in the steeple of Old
North Church to signal Paul Revere that the
British expeditionary force was coming by sea.
Revere rode toward Lexington by way of
Charlestown neck to warn Sam Adams and John
Hancock, as well as the countryside, of the British
Regular's march on Lexington and Concord.

Freedom Trail Guide

The Freedom Trail consists of a three-mile trail that
highlights sixteen historic sites within downtown
Boston and Charlestown.

Park Street Church

Park Street Church is located on the corner of Park
and Tremont Streets, across from Boston Common.
Constructed in 1809, it was once referred to as
"Brimstone Corner" where gunpowder for the War
of 1812 was stored in a crypt in the basement of the
church. Here vendors sell t-shirts along the street.

ABOVE

Park Street Church

The cornerstone of this congregational church was laid on May 1, 1809. The striking steeple rises 217 feet to its weathervane.

OPPOSITE

Hancock Towers

The old and new Hancock Towers as viewed across the lagoon in the Public Gardens. The mirrored glass finish of the new Hancock Tower erected in 1976 reflects the image of the 1947 Old John Hancock Tower.

Worcester Square Fountain Statue

Worcester Square Park is a beautiful little park in Boston's South End.

South End Entry

Bright varnished oak doors with brass trim and black wrought iron rails distinguish the entry to this South End home.

Christopher Columbus Park

This waterfront park is located on Atlantic Avenue between Long and Commercial Wharves in Boston's North End. The park provides excellent views of Boston's inner harbor.

Boston Common Baseball

Little League Baseball is just one of many events taking place on the Common on a spring afternoon.

Mounted Police

The Boston Police Mounted Unit was established in 1883. Mounted police provide a highly mobile force with great visibility. The horses are carefully selected for a calm temperament in crowds and traffic.

The Partisans

Andrzei Pitynski's 1979 tribute to guerilla freedom fighters everywhere is located in the Boston Commons.

Christian Science Center

The world headquarters of the Christian Science Church located at 175 Huntington Avenue is known as the "Mother Church." Established in Boston by Mary Baker Eddy in 1879, it is home to the fascinating Mapparium; a thirty-foot stained glass globe that visitors view from a glass catwalk dissecting the interior of the globe.

LEFT

Prudential Center Statue

This bronze statue situated on the Prudential Plaza appears to take flight.

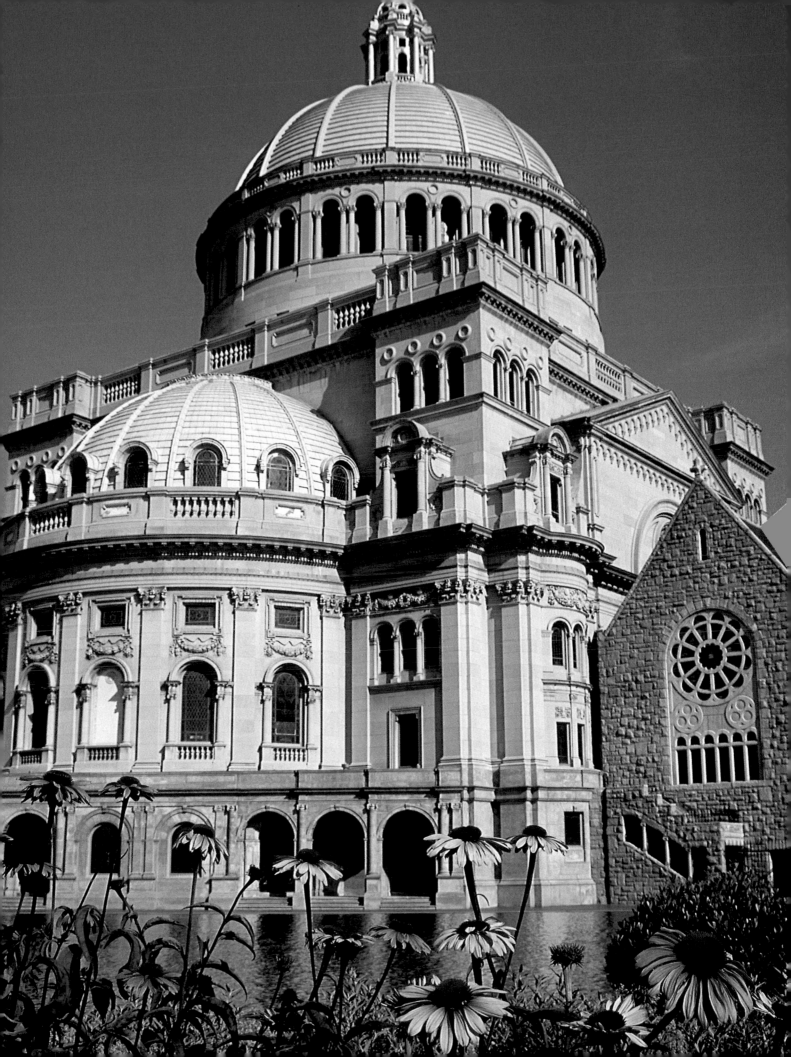

Charles Street Post Office

This picture captures the old world feeling of the
architecture along Charles Street.

Hopkinton, 26.2 Miles to Finish

The Boston Marathon begins in Hopkinton; 26.2
miles west of Boston. The finish line opposite
Copley Square is a welcome site to the thousands of
runners who finish the race every Patriot's Day.

Chart House

The Chart House Restaurant located on Long Warf provides a great place to view the waterfront from while enjoying excellent seafood.

ABOVE

Fenway Score Board

Boston Red Sox Manny Ramirez stands guard in
Fenway's left field. The scoreboard at the base of the
Green Monster shows the Sox off to an early lead
against their rivals the NY Yankees.

LEFT

Red Sox

The Boston Red Sox are near and dear to the
Fenway Faithful.

ABOVE

Yawkey Way

Fenway Park was first opened on April 20, 1912 and it hasn't changed much since then The Red Sox provide public tours of the park on a daily basis.

LEFT

Sausage King

Vendors outside of Fenway Park hawk everything from Cracker-Jacks, peanuts, ball caps and banners to sweet sausage and sweatshirts.

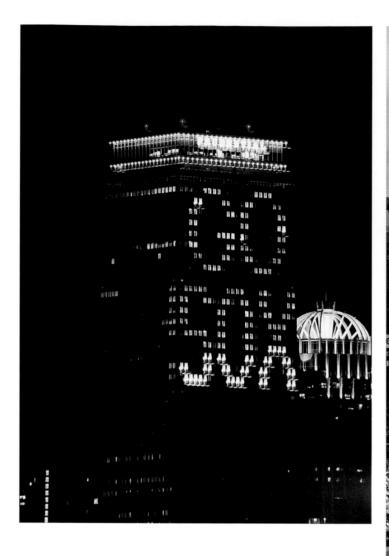

Towering Support

The Prudential Tower shows its support for Red
Sox baseball.

Fenway Park

Red Sox short stop Nomar Garciaparra watches
from the on-deck circle as team mate Johnny
Damon steals second.

ABOVE AND RIGHT

The Feast of St. Anthony

Boston's North End celebrates the Feast of St.
Anthony at the end of August each year. This festival has been celebrated here since 1919.

BOSTON: A PHOTOGRAPHIC PORTRAIT 57

Italian Serenade

An accordion player along Hanover Street in the
North End celebrates during an Italian-American
Festival.

The Majestic

Owned by Emerson College the ornate Majestic
Theatre on Tremont Street was built in 1903.
Public tours are available on most Fridays.

Fountains

Reflecting pools at the Christian Science Center come to life with their exquisite fountains and decorative lighting.

Mayor Curley

Boston is a city that loves its statues. This bronze of
Mayor Curley located opposite Faneuil Hall depicts
the fiery politician who served four terms as
Boston's mayor.

Union Oyster House

Established in 1826, The Union Oyster House is a
Boston landmark and the oldest restaurant in the
city. The building itself is more than 250 years old.

Faneuil Hall Marketplace

The marketplace has played a central role in Boston history for over 250 years. It now hosts dozens of food stalls and shops purveying everything from postcards and t-shirts to New England Clam Chowder.

ABOVE

Emmets Pub

Emmets of Boston at 6 Beacon Street is a fine Irish
Pub worth a visit.

LEFT

Beacon Street

This is a typical Beacon Hill entry with its granite
steps, black wrought iron railings, planters and
stately doorway.

OPPOSITE

Acorn Street

Narrow cobble stoned Beacon Hill Lanes lit by gas
street lights and decorated with window boxes can
be found throughout the area.

ABOVE

Ladder Truck

This classic firehouse on Boylston Street was built in 1887 to house both fire and police stations. It was renovated in 1976 and no longer houses the police station.

LEFT

Samuel Adams Gravesite

Samuel Adams was a vocal and active revolutionary. He protested the stamp act, founded the Sons of Liberty, devised the plan for the Boston Tea Party and signed the declaration of independence. He died in 1803 and is buried in the Granary Burying Ground.

OPPOSITE

Christopher Columbus Park

These 340 foot-long arched trellises are covered with leafy vines that lead from the waterfront toward the Custom House Tower and Faneuil Hall Marketplace

ABOVE

Piers Park

Piers Park in East Boston was designed with a great
deal of community input. The 1995 project
reclaimed piers and created an amphitheatre, breath-
taking access to the waterfront and recreation space
for the community.

RIGHT

East Boston Waterfront

The Boston skyline as viewed from an East Boston
marina.

Quincy Market

Quincy Market was constructed in 1825 to serve as
Boston's wholesale food marketplace. Today it is a
shopping destination for tens of thousands. City
licensed street performers entertain visitors. These
performers compete by audition for the limited
permits available.

South Station

South Station terminal, constructed in 1899, was once the world's largest. It was touted for its underground tracks which would allow passengers to board trains in the safety and comfort of indoors.

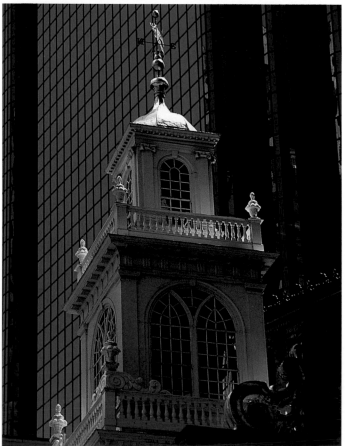

Surging Fountain

The fountain at Christopher Columbus Park along
the waterfront in the North End is near the Rose
Kennedy Gardens.

Old State House

Boston's oldest public building, the Old State
House, was constructed in 1713. It sits on the corner of State and Washington Streets, opposite the
site of the Boston Massacre of March 5, 1770.
The building is open for tours.

Old North Church Steeple

Christ Church of Boston is the oldest church in the
city having been constructed in 1723. Its 191 foot-
tall steeple is the tallest in the city and was the site
of the two signal lanterns placed to signal patriot
Paul Revere.

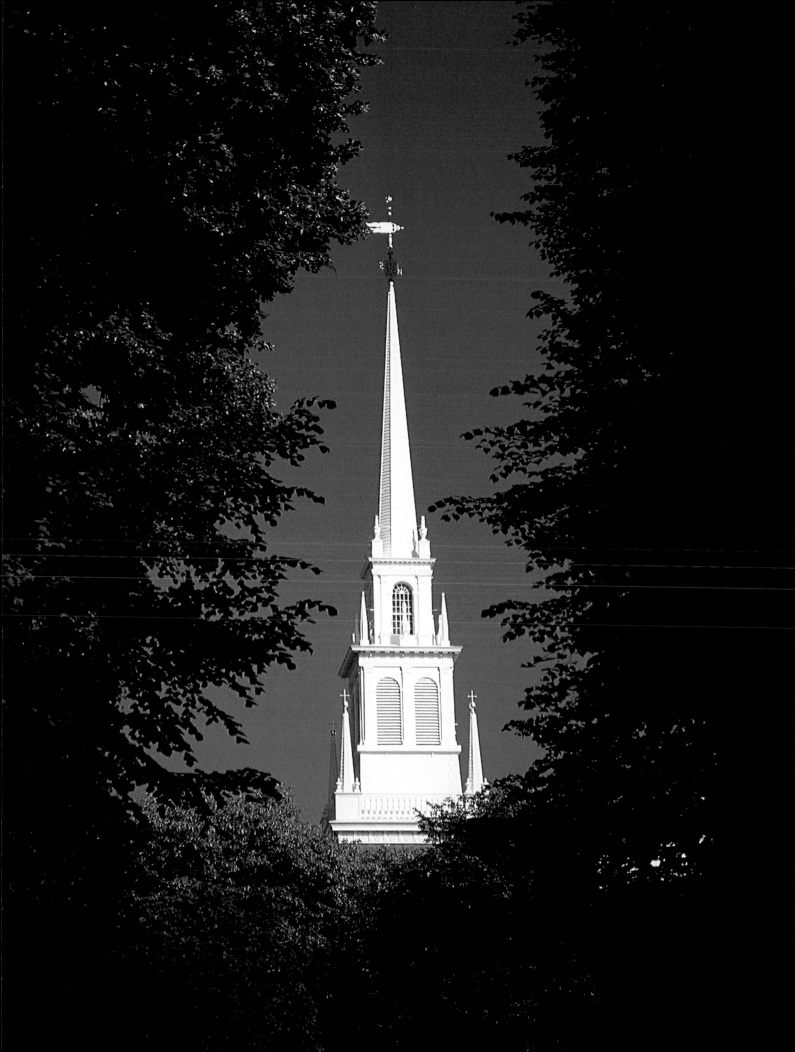

Horse and Carriage

A Hansom Cab and its steed at Quincy Market await riders for a city tour.

Old State House Balcony

The Declaration of Independence was first read to Boson residents from this porch on July 18, 1776. Soon after the proclamation the Lion and Unicorn, emblems of British Royalty, disappeared. They were later restored in 1882.

State House Unicorn

Close-up of Unicorn and cupola atop the Old State House.

LEFT AND RIGHT

Middlesex County Volunteers

The Middlesex County Volunteers are a Fife and Drum Corp who perform music from the 17th through early 19th centuries in period dress.

OPPOSITE

Old City Hall

Located at 45 School Street, Old City Hall, a French Second Empire Style building, was completed in 1865 and served as Boston's City Hall until 1969. Today it is occupied by offices and a restaurant.

Children's Museum

The Boston Children's Museum at 300 Congress
Street utilizes interactive exhibits to make learning
fun and interesting for children.

Tea Party

The brig Beaver II is a replica of one of the three
original tea party ships that Sam Adams and his
friends boarded dressed as Indians to dump the
taxed tea into the harbor.

Sea Buscuit

On June 29, 1936 Sea Biscuit was discovered at Suffolk Downs by trainer Tom Smith. The statue in this picture is a monument to the horse and to jockey Red Pallard.

And the Winner Is...

Horses round the track at East Boston's Suffolk
Downs. The park was built in 1935 and was
Massachusetts' first major race track.

John F. Kennedy Library

The JFK Library and museum is dedicated to the memory of our thirty-fifth president. It's located on Columbia Point and sees some 200,000 visitors annually.

Sloop Victura

The Victura was a gift to fifteen year old JFK from his parents and remained one of his prized possessions throughout his life.

Power Walk

Christopher Columbus Park is close to Boston's financial district and North End. Close enough for a quick stroll through the park after lunch.

John F. Kennedy Library

The JFK Library contains over 8.4 millions pages of
President Kennedy's papers and some 180,000 still
photographs. The complex contains approximately
173,000 square feet divided between the library and
museum.

ABOVE

JFK / Nixon Debate Studio

Visitors can view a recreation of the studio where
their famous debate took place. Excerpts of the
actual debates are played on the monitors.

LEFT

Jaqueline Kennedy's Wedding Dress

The First Lady's wedding gown is made from fifty
yards of ivory silk taffeta that has been carefully
preserved by the Textile Conservation Center of
Lowell. The dress required two months to create.

Holocaust Memorial

These six etched glass towers are located near the
Faneuil Hall Marketplace. Each of the towers
represents one of the six Nazi concentration camps:
Auschwitz-Birkenau, Belzec, Chelmno, Majdanek,
Sobibor and Treblinka. Six million numbers are
etched into the glass suggesting the tattooed numbers used in the Nazi death camps. Over 3000
organizations worked toward the 1995 dedication
of this memorial.

ABOVE

John Joseph Moakley U. S. Courthouse

The federal courthouse is situated on Fan Pier in South Boston. Its award winning design features a 375 foot-long by 88 foot-high wall of glass.

LEFT

Boston Harbor Hotel

The Terrace provides a wonderful dining experience beside Boston's active harbor. During the summer months the hotel transforms this terrace into an outdoor cinema for the Movies by Moonlight Series.

Long View

The trellis on the left frames this view of
Christopher Columbus Park with the Custom
House Tower dominating the focus of the shot.

ABOVE

Moakley Bridge

Evelyn Moakley Bridge provides access to South Boston across the Fort Point Channel.

LEFT

Water Front

Waterfront property in Boston once included the Custom House Tower in the background of this view. As more real estate was required, land was filled and buildings erected.

Chinatown Archway

The large Chinese characters on this ornate arch
read "Welcome to All." Established around 1900,
Boston's Chinatown is the third oldest in the country.

Chinatown Mural

There are four community murals in Chinatown.
Each tells its own story.

Community Gardens, Chinatown

The Chinatown gardens are available to residents who gain great satisfaction and enjoyment from farming their plots. Each garden is unique and reflects the personality of its owner. Many grow vegetables while some choose to nurture flowers.

Copley Square Fountains

The fountains at Copley Square were part of the 1976 renovation of the park and are an inviting place to spend a lunch hour.

LEFT

Copley Square Statue

A statue of John Singleton Copley, for whom the square is named, stands watch. Copley was an accomplished Boston artist. More than fifty of his works are on display at the Museum of Fine Arts.

RIGHT

Swan

The swans in the public gardens have a soothing affect, but don't get too close!

OPPOSITE

Boston Light

Boston Light, located on Little Brewster Island, is the oldest lighthouse in the country. The rope labyrinth in the image is used by the civilian light keeper to assist her in focusing during her morning yoga meditation.

Tugboats

This picture, taken from atop the Bunker Hill Monument, gives you a birds eye view of a fleet of tugboats and oilers tied up at the Boston Fuel Transportation Dock.

Firefighter

Boston's fireboat *Firefighter* is used for celebrations, greeting visiting vessels, but its primary duty is protecting the waterfront. Here she is shown docked at Burroughs Wharf.

Leonard P. Zakim Bunker Hill Bridge

This $100,000,000 bridge carries route I-93 in and out of the Boston's Big Dig Tunnel beneath the city. The tops of the towers are designed to replicate the image of the Bunker Hill Monument. Colored lighting at night creates a spectacular sight.

Morning on the Charles River

The John Hancock Building towers over the Boston skyline as seen from the Cambridge side of the Charles River.

ABOVE

Aquarium Voyager III

Voyager II & III are operated by the New England Aquarium for whale watches. They depart Central Wharf and utilize their fast catamaran design to quickly carry passengers out to whales.

LEFT

New England Aquarium

The New England Aquarium on Central Wharf first opened its doors in 1969. Their centerpiece is the giant ocean tank that rises through the center of the building and contains 200,000 gallons of salt water.

OPPOSITE

Waterboat Marina

Lobster buoys hang from the fence around the marina located on Long Wharf in front of Quincy Market.

Boston Light

Boston Light stands 98 feet above Little Brewster Island, which is connected by a sandbar to Great Brewster Island. Its beacon is visible for twenty-seven miles. The original tower was built in 1716 but was heavily damaged during the revolutionary war by both the British and the Colonists. It was rebuilt in 1783.

Boat tours that visit the island are available.

Whale Watching

A pair of humpbacks break the surface alongside the whale watch boat Yankee Freedom out of Gloucester Harbor. Most whale watch companies guarantee whale sightings.

Seaport Belle, Boston Harbor

The sixty-two foot steamboat replica, Seaport Belle, is operated by Mass Bay Lines and is available for harbor tours.

Humpback Whale

The flukes of this humpback whale are visible as she begins to dive. These whales live on a diet of krill and small fish. They can consume up to 1.5 tons of food per day.

Georges Island

Tours from Long Wharf carry visitors to Ft. Warren
on Georges Island. This fort was constructed in
1833 to protect the entrance to Boston Harbor.

Little Brewster Island

Little Brewster Island is the site of Boston Light and
its light keeper's house. The keeper's house was constructed in 1884.

ABOVE

USS Constitution Museum

The USS Constitution Museum is along the
Freedom Trail. Its interactive displays are an interesting and fun path to learning about the life and
times of the *Constitution*. Admission is free.

OPPOSITE

Skyline through the Rigging

The Custom House Tower is a relative new-comer
to the Boston skyline when compared to frigate
Constitution which was launched and christened
with a bottle of Madeira wine in 1794.

Constitution Turn-Around

The *USS Constitution* is taken by tugboat out into
the harbor for semi-annual turn-arounds and special
events. It was nicknamed *Old Ironsides* from the war
of 1812 when it is said that British shot bounced off
her sides.

Tobin Bridge

The double deck Tobin Bridge spans Route One across the Mystic River. This view is north from Charlestown toward Chelsea and the North Shore. Container ships dock at the piers in the foreground.

U.S.S. Constitution, Charlestown

In her berth below the Bunker Hill Monument the oldest commissioned ship in the United States Navy is open to visitors year round. The copper sheathing that protects the hull of the ship was created and applied by coppersmith Paul Revere.

LEFT

Colonel Prescott

Colonel William Prescott led the colonials in the Battle of Bunker Hill. The majority of fighting actually took place on Breeds Hill where Prescott had his men dig fortifications throughout the night. Although the battle was lost when the patriots ran out of ammunition it did prove that the British had their hands full. This monument is located on Bunker Hill, Charlestown.

OPPOSITE

Harvard University

The Harvard University clock tower in Cambridge.

Night Time Skyline

An evening view of the Boston skyline across the
Charles River.

Independence Day

Boston's spectacular Fourth of July Fireworks has
been touted as "America's biggest Independence
Day party" where nearly 400,000 people have
attended this celebration in recent years. This thirty-
minute fireworks display ignites some ten thousand
pyrotechnic shells and devices and requires over
eight days to construct, load and wire.

Leonard P. Zakim Bridge

Boston's newest bridge at night and at sunrise. One hundred and sixteen cables support the roadway from the two hollow, concrete A-frame towers that rise 322 feet and 295 feet respectively to compensate for grade running down into the tunnel.

Custom House Tower

The Custom House Tower was Boston's first
skyscraper and was at one time located on the
waterfront. The tower never moved but filling of
the shoreline moved the waterfront.

Salute to the Troops

Boaters crowd the Charles River Basin to view the
Independence Day celebration.

Wadsworth House

The Wadsworth house was completed in 1727 and is the oldest building in Harvard Square. George Washington slept here and it has served as residence to Harvard presidents, students and administrators.

Out of Town News

Out of Town News at the kiosk at Harvard Square sells newspapers and magazines from around the world.

First Parish Church

The statue of Charles Sumner sits before the First Parish in Harvard Square. Sculptor Ann Whitney's design of the statue was rejected when it was discovered that the sculptor was a women, and the commission was withheld. In her eighties she funded the statue herself and donated it to the city.

Mount Auburn Cemetery

The Mount Auburn Cemetery spans the border
between Cambridge and Watertown and dates back
to 1831. This experimental garden started by the
Massachusetts Horticultural Society was to become
the first garden cemetery in this country.

ABOVE

Runners Along the Charles

Warm weather brings out the leaves and the
runners along Memorial Drive beside the
Charles River.

OPPOSITE

Mount Auburn Cemetery

Mount Auburn Cemetery comprises over 175 acres
and has been designated a National Historic
Landmark. It is recognized as one of this countries
significant designed landscapes.

ABOVE

Rowers at Weeks Bridge

Women's eights pause beneath the Weeks Bridge as
they take a break from their training on the Charles
River.

OPPOSITE

The Coop

A student group founded the Harvard/MIT
Cooperative Society in 1882 to establish a location
for professionals and academics to purchase merchandise at competitive prices.

Kevin, Susan and Jessica Psaros

While primarily known for their nature photography, the Psaros' welcomed the opportunity to expand their photographic horizons by collaborating on this book. They currently reside in Groveland, MA with their three-year-old daughter Jessica, who often accompanied them on their photo treks to Boston.

Kevin and Susan have established a Fine Art and Stock Photography business and have exhibited their award winning photographs in numerous local venues as well as being published both locally and nationally. They have contributed to previous Photographic Series books by Twin Lights Publishers.

Print inquiries and comments may be directed to:
Kevin and Susan Psaros
9 Groveland Commons Way
Groveland, MA 01834
psaros@comcast.net
www.natureartists.com/psarosks.htm